THE ENIGMA OF
THE SUICIDE BOMBER

THE ENIGMA OF THE SUICIDE BOMBER

A Psychoanalytic Essay

Franco De Masi

Translated by Philip Slotkin

KARNAC

First published in Italian as *Trauma, deumanizzazione e distruttività* in 2008 by © Franco Angeli s.r.l., Milan.

First English edition published in 2011 by
Karnac Books Ltd
118 Finchley Road, London NW3 5HT

British Library Cataloguing in Publication Data

A C.I.P. for this book is available from the British Library

ISBN: 978 1 85575 822 3

Translated by Philip Slotkin

Edited, designed and produced by The Studio Publishing Services Ltd
www.publishingservicesuk.co.uk
e-mail: studio@publishingservicesuk.co.uk

Printed in Great Britain

www.karnacbooks.com

CONTENTS

ACKNOWLEDGEMENTS

I wish to thank Claudio Fasoli, Angela Ulianova Radice, Paolo Schettino, and Ivana Suhadolc for suggestions that have made this book more complete and more readable.

Franco De Masi is a training analyst of the Italian Psychoanalytical Society and former President of the Centro Milanese di Psicoanalisi and Secretary of the Training Institute of Milan. He is a medical doctor and a psychiatrist who has worked for many years in psychiatric hospitals. During the past thirty years, he has been working as a full-time psychoanalyst in Milan. His main interests have been focused on the theoretical and technical psychoanalytical issues related to severely ill or psychotic patients.

And Samson called unto the Lord, and said, O Lord God, remember me, I pray thee, and strengthen me, I pray thee, only this once, O God, that I may be at once avenged of the Philistines for my two eyes. And Samson took hold of the two middle pillars upon which the house stood, and on which it was borne up, of the one with his right hand, and of the other with his left. And Samson said, Let me die with the Philistines. And he bowed himself with all his might; and the house fell upon the lords, and upon all the people that were therein. So the dead which he slew at his death were more than they which he slew in his life. [Judges 16: 28–33]

The only way out of the dilemma is to fuse destruction and self-destruction, aggression and auto-aggression. On the one hand, at the moment of his explosion, the loser for once experiences a feeling of true power. His act allows him to triumph over others by annihilating them. And on the other, he does justice to the reverse of this feeling of power, the suspicion that his own existence might be worthless, by putting an end to it. [Enzensberger, 2005]

Anna Maria Nicolò

Can psychoanalysts concern themselves with momentous social and political phenomena such as terrorism? What instruments do analysts have at their disposal to respond to the myriad questions which they pose? In this book, Franco De Masi implicitly sets himself this challenge and bravely confronts it, offering us a forceful, eloquent, and at the same time fascinating account. He presents us with an initial exploration of a difficult terrain whose features are both unknown and contradictory; there is never a moment of tedium, and the narrative unfolds like a novel or thriller that is impossible to put down, as we anticipate the final outcome page after page.

In following the development of Franco De Masi's ideas, the reader will almost unwittingly begin to reflect on issues that sometimes impress and sometimes escape him[1]—issues to which one is, nevertheless, inevitably exposed, bombarded as we all are by media coverage.

Yet, this volume extends over a wide range of highly important subject matter. The first part deals with the relative roles of religion, gender, and sociopolitical processes as factors underlying terrorist acts. In the second part, the author reflects on the concepts of victimization and dehumanization; while, in the third, he enquires into the nature of the terrorist's mental functioning.

On the basis of his many references, but in particular by virtue of the ideas he develops, Dr De Masi ultimately reaches the important conclusion that the phenomenon of terrorism cannot be understood in terms solely of the individual. The specific element involved in terrorism is stated to be the "pathological union of individual suffering with the omnipotent, destructive mentality of the political or religious organization". Apart from the associated political and social considerations, these notions open the way to a wide-ranging and interesting field for research, which may even lead us to take a new look at many of the more serious pathologies that at present leave us powerless and unprepared. These pathologies cannot in my view be seen as affecting individual minds only, but can justly be described as transpersonal. The attention devoted in recent times to transgenerational phenomena is but one example among many.

However, all human functioning may be said to involve a transpersonal level that must be taken seriously, even if it admittedly comes particularly to the fore in severe or extreme situations. Psychoanalysts from Janine Puget to Isidoro Berenstein, and from René Kaës to Silvia Amati Sas, to mention only a few, have focused increasingly on these forms of functioning.

In an interesting and subtle contribution on traumatic social violence and the problem of our defensive adaptation to it, Dr Amati Sas (2002), taking Bleger's psychoanalytic theories as her starting point, describes the case of a female patient who was abducted by the Argentine military and subjected to various kinds of violence and torture. She concludes that traumatic violence results in regression to a state of ambiguity, in which the victim becomes malleable and susceptible, thus enabling the torturer to gain entry to her internal world and occupy the place of the privileged objects within it. These mechanisms usurp and sabotage the "identificatory project" (Aulagnier, 1986) and the subject's ideal of moral functioning.

As we know—and as Dr De Masi shows with a plethora of examples—the apprentice terrorist is progressively isolated from his original environment, joining a new group where he ultimately undergoes comprehensive acculturation, and in which, in particular, he lapses into a state of regressive dependence on the "master" and the group itself. There comes a point when he loses his natural bearings; he is no longer even master of his own body, so that his level of uncertainty increases, and (as Bleger would contend) must therefore immediately seek in the environment a depository for the "ambiguous nucleus"—that is, for the most undifferentiated parts of the self.

Normal people too—indeed, especially normal people—unconsciously adapt to their environment and remodel themselves in accordance with it. In situations of stress, alarm, or peril such as those currently afflicting various parts of the world, manipulation is a natural state of affairs because "the transsubjective space is thoroughly imprecise and ambiguous, so that one tends to accept even what would normally be unacceptable" (Amati Sas, 2002, translated for this publication).

This regressive dimension is discussed in detail by Dr De Masi, and the reader reflects with him on how the blurring of the distinction between self and other contributes to the causation of phenomena such as suicide terrorism.

This kind of regressive functioning closely resembles that observed in couples or families who exhibit violent behaviour, as well as in adolescent gangs; however, as Vamir Volkan (2003) points out, it is also seen in large groups in the aftermath of a traumatic event affecting an entire society.

It would be interesting to consider in depth what exactly we mean by the term "trauma", and Dr De Masi mentions some of its possible connotations in psychoanalytic theory. The concept of trauma is then found to be inseparable from that of identity.

We live in an age in which our identities are sorely tried not only by the disturbing relationship with the alien and unknown "other", but also by the speed and frequency of information and by the media's particular concentration on catastrophes; all these factors call into question the security of our allegiances and ideas.

As the author reminds us, we all have before our eyes the insistent images of the collapsing Twin Towers on 9/11. These events shook the security of our world to its foundations, bearing witness to the crisis afflicting the bedrock elements, or "meta-social guarantors" (Touraine, 1997; Kaës, 2005)—such as myths, ideologies, beliefs, religion, authority, and hierarchy—of our social and cultural lives.

The reaction to these events is a crisis of identity. The response to 9/11 was the short-circuit of war, a solution that had many advantages: consolidating the group around an ideal and a leader; offering an explanation for the unexplainable, as a kind of pseudo-working through; and, as Amati Sas (2002, translated) puts it, offering "a symbolic depository which, while shared, is sufficiently concrete and seemingly known". All this enables us to cling to our known identity and thereby somehow re-establishes our internal and external world.

However, can the mere threat to identity resulting from a traumatic situation, even if severe and repeated, account for the creation of a terrorist and for a sacrificial state of mind? This is another of the questions posed in the book, and once again Dr De Masi draws attention to the complexity of the factors involved in this situation. The processes of idealization and total submission are among his suggested answers.

As the author tells us, apart from their horrific act of violence, terrorists lead normal lives, are educated normally, and have normal interests and families; such persons cannot be classified in any diagnostic category, and indeed our customary diagnostic categories are inapplicable to them.

This is in fact not the first time we have had to alter our reference parameters or techniques—we have done so, for instance, when working with concentration camp survivors, with patients who have suffered multiple traumas or who exhibit severe forms of criminality or psychopathy, and more recently with paedophiles. As psychoanalysts, we are increasingly endeavouring to put ourselves in Cain's shoes, and destructiveness is increasingly assuming unprecedented dimensions that we are as yet unable to confront. We have come to realize that every individual is not only the witness but also the unconscious agent of such violence, and for this reason we are becoming more and more aware that our field is not confined to the internal world of the individual, but extends to all aspects of the relationship between the intrapsychic and the interpersonal.

Of course, we cannot presume to offer a psychoanalytic explanation for all events, including those on the sociopolitical stage, determined as they are by a large number of factors, many of them unknown and therefore beyond our understanding. Although we are unable to accommodate them in the framework of a diagnosis, we must be aware of the scientific and moral necessity of observing these realities too and of attempting with due humility to comprehend them. After all, in the words of Puget (1995), they too are "psychoanalytic material".

The reader of this slim volume will find himself in the company of an analyst with vast clinical experience, especially with patients at the limit of treatability, an analyst curious about the world around him, and an analyst dedicated to teaching the upcoming generation, as he embarks on a pioneering exploration of this as yet unknown territory from a variety of perspectives.

Daniel Pick

As I read the psychoanalyst Franco De Masi's book during December 2010, the newspapers carried daily updates on suicide bombings. His text could scarcely have been more timely. One item told of a botched mission in Stockholm; another of thirteen dead and dozens injured after an explosion had ripped through a Christmas market in the Philippine city of General Santos. Still another reported mass casualties in Pakistan, under the heading, "Attack from what is believed to be the first female suicide bomber in country strikes food centre and injures over 100" (*Guardian*, 12 and 13 December 2010; *Guardian* website, 25 December 2010.). Yet more reports from around the globe soon followed, as though sombrely punctuating each chapter of his enquiry. Over the years, there have been thousands of deaths from such suicide missions. Whatever the variable risk of fatality for modern city-dwellers and travellers, in different times and places, the endless cycle of suicide missions suggests the depth of current crises around the globe and the nebulous nature of the so-called war against terror that was launched in order to restore "order" some years ago. These missions have become the methodology of choice for diverse insurgencies, waging battle in situations of asymmetric power. Social scientists endeavour to find the common threads in such campaigns; but they also reveal the multiplicity of distinct histories, conflicts and concerns out of which they grow (Cf. Diego Gambetta (Ed.), *Making Sense of Suicide Missions*, Oxford, 2005.).

De Masi is clearly not in two minds about the horror of suicide missions, nor of the importance of defending liberty and democracy (in so far as they may exist). He is not interested, however, in ritual denunciation. Rather he tries to imagine the inner world of those who conduct or organize such indiscriminate bombings in order to effect change on behalf of non-governmental organizations. Eschewing knee-jerk accounts of the necessary mental deficiency and psychopathy of the perpetrators, he initiates a more complicated reflection as to what psychosocial circumstances pull certain people towards such choices.

What is communicated through the violence in these outrages? Sacrificial wishes, perhaps; murderous consequences, to be sure; but also, he surmises (on the basis of the testimony he has consulted) a transfer of emotions and experiences, such as rage, humiliation, impotence, grief or grievance. It is also true that calculated political purposes are inherent in such actions, not just, or perhaps not even primarily, emotionally inchoate or incontinent feelings. Each action addresses, or in some eyes, redresses, earlier wrongs: one person's terrorist is not only another's freedom fighter but also another's counter-terrorist.

De Masi examines the nature of this path from subjective doubt to utter certainty, and from live feelings of connection with and passion for the other to the cut-off state of mind that is required. A cool head is to be preferred in order for the agent to be capable of completing the mission reliably. How is this state secured? In the 1950s, this process might have been described simply enough as "brainwashing". Evidently, a more complex kind of interaction is involved, and a less one-dimensional vocabulary is required even to begin to consider it. One question is how particular organizations and/or the legitimating higher "spiritual" authority manage to trump all other affective claims upon the subject. The other is how the subject is drawn, consciously and unconsciously, to this "higher" calling in the first place. In short what kinds of interpersonal and intrapsychic exchange are required to seal the dire process that De Masi calls "dehumanization"?

One way into such matters is through the recent feature film to which De Masi refers—*Paradise Now*, directed by the Palestinian exile Hany Abu-Assad. It tracks a forty-eight-hour period in the life of two friends. Said and Khaled, it turns out, have already decided to act, in the face of personal shame, as well as hardships, countless frustrations, intense feelings of provocation and the general destitution and emptiness of their life in the territories. We see life from their point of view, as they are penned in by fences, jams and menacing blockades. Considering the potential outcome of their action, they fluctuate between the wild hope that it will secure a transformation and resignation to the fact that it will not. Yet utility is not necessarily the point.

The film examines the existential choices that emerge before and after the organization to which they have pledged themselves decrees that it is time for them to die and to kill. The drama is whether, like self-styled Antigones, they will go through to the end, despite the increasingly desperate ministrations of a friend (herself made fatherless through such martyrdom).Once the mission is set in place, their work is to be *silent* and steadfast; family and friends are kept in ignorance, discussion reduced to a minimum, rituals of preparation passed through. In fact, things go awry before their first mission is carried out and the focus of the film turns to the consequences of their subsequent confusion when the chance for "second thoughts" arises.

De Masi explores the interplay between the subject's inner struggle, the culture and thought of the organization they serve, and the ravaged social and political landscape around them. *Paradise Now* hinges on the unexpected opportunity to double back. In the plot of the film it turns out that *either* going forward *or* turning back is immensely problematic for the protagonists. De Masi pays particular attention to the moment when one of these volunteers (in the turmoil of the failure of the first mission) lies prostrate on the grave of his father, a man who had been executed for his collaboration with the Israelis.

The volunteer's mind is supposed to be steeled, while the adversary is to be traumatized and filled with doubt. Certain terrorist organizations, De Masi writes, aim "to strike indiscriminately, to arouse anxiety, and to confuse and disorientate the target group". For this to occur, there has to be a survivor, even perhaps a majority of survivors, who can witness and be viscerally affected. This account is in one sense a response to 9/11, but not only that, since, as he points out, analogous, deliberately designed catastrophes have occurred elsewhere. There are other situations where bombs have crashed through major public buildings, or where observers have had to witness the moment of the missile strike. There is a point (perhaps 9/11 was one of these) in which the entire cultural framework within which we collectively manage anxiety threatens to totter and fall; in psychoanalytic terms, there are moments in which "the container" (for Bion) or "the symbolic order" (for Lacan) founders and even threatens momentarily to collapse altogether (assuming we were sane enough for it to have existed in the first place).

The Enigma uses clinical and historical vignettes to examine how thought is hollowed out and alternatives foreclosed; like the film above, it seeks to understand how and why this occurs. The author helps us to see the multiply determined nature of the decision and the interaction of self and other. This has affinities with the way psychoanalysts today might look not just at the patient's pathology, but rather at the *enactment* that can remorselessly ensue between the two parties, and in which perception *and misperception* operate at many different levels.

When psychic and social order is reconstituted after trauma, "ours" or "theirs", it often has a harder edge. The American administration's aggressive military follow-up to the disaster (whose epicentre was Manhattan) is a case in point. But such policy was not, however, simply an expression of raw emotion, in response to the violent outrage; still less was it anything resembling a wise long-term programme of effectual action, thought-through, "in the depressive position".

Whatever the post mortem on the original policy of invasion in Afghanistan or, very differently, in Iraq, it is clear how little has been satisfactorily resolved, even within the *Realpolitik* calculations of the original architects. Tears need not be shed about the ousted regimes in either case, but the manner in which "our" political decisions were arrived at in the first place (and public opinion manipulated, especially in relation to Iraq) to secure consent is a still-smouldering scandal, at least in Britain.

To take a leaf out of De Masi's book, psychoanalysis *should* have a place in this discussion, not only because of the psychopathology and terrifying charismatic "certainty" of individual leaders, but because of the disturbing, often supine functioning of the group (in the case of the UK, for example, the Cabinet that takes collective responsibility for government policy). The psychoanalysis of groups might help us understand better the organizational pathology that dominated Anglo-American policy at large. The fall-out from the Twin Tower disaster was enormously complicated and painful, but its *usage* was blunt and, at least at one level, transparent. But inevitably it backfired. Who can forget the supreme moment of false reassurance: that narcissistic display of the quintessential Oedipal son, George W. Bush, piloting his own plane on to the vast aircraft carrier and proclaiming "mission accomplished"?

De Masi reminds us that neither the willingness to bomb non-combatants, nor to die for a sacred cause, nor even to turn planes into missiles is new; but in our own time, suicide missions have become associated, above all, with religious fundamentalism and fanaticism, although they are carried out by people with secular outlooks too. Such headings, he also reminds us, do not take the discussion very far, and often elide the specific campaigns and political objectives of insurrectionary movements. What is clear is that suicide missions pose an enormous challenge to conventional security forces, however powerful. The psychological dynamics are complex, although the technical means are relatively simple. Still more terrible forms of destruction lurk in the future, but thus far, as Mike Davis describes in his history of the car bomb, *Buda's Wagon* (2007), it is neither stealthily concealed nuclear devices nor anthrax that have bedevilled life in Beirut, Kabul, Islamabad, Jerusalem, Baghdad or for that matter New York, but rather, conventional weapons and well-worn techniques, used in clandestine ways.

Slaughter in New York and, on a lesser scale, in London and Madrid, brought the crisis home to us in the West; bloodshed in Moscow took the Chechen morass back to the Russia capital. The latest plots in Stockholm and Copenhagen sent further reminders that no city can be sure it is immune. Suicide bombers have proved ever more adroit at turning transportation—cars, buses, lorries and trains, as well as the body itself—into moving bombs. Powerful states and armies struggle to respond to the threat.

The destruction of the World Trade Center (the starting point of De Masi's account) may not have marked an epochal shift, but it demonstrated how much had changed in the standard tactics of terror; in place of "mere" hijacking or targeted attacks, the *desire* for wanton slaughter. The social and political origins of current counter-insurgency practices can be debated. It was perhaps the Italian anarchist militant, Mario Buda (the point of departure in Mike Davis' concise and telling book, which is to be recommended as complementary reading alongside De Masi's psychoanalytical study), who provided inspiration for later car bombers, when he planted a wagon with explosives in Wall Street in September 1920 and walked away: fire, deaths, injuries, mountains of rubble, general mayhem, and panic duly resulted.

Despite some earlier precedents (notably by Fenians and anarchists in Victorian times), Buda's wagon, Davis argues, marked the beginning of the history of a new kind of weaponry, albeit, at this stage, without a determinedly suicidal driver on board. Further refinements of technology, technique and attitude were soon to follow in the very different social and political circumstances of our own times. Buda had in fact, escaped to his native Romagna, where, rumour had it, he became a spy for Mussolini. Seven months after the Wall Street bombing of 1920, Catalan anarcho-syndicalists provided a motorized version of this device, as part of a campaign that resulted, *inter alia*, in numerous deaths in Barcelona and its surrounding area.

One problem with much media discussion of terrorism and suicide bombing is the assumption of absolute novelty and the sense that what is occurring is some scandalous aberration from the "norm". It would be as absurd to claim that *nothing* has changed as to insist that everything has been turned upside down by, say, 9/11. The nature of what has changed requires clarification since suicidal acts in war and conflict, or, for that matter the willingness of states and of non-state organizations to target civilians has a much longer reach. De Masi casts an eye back to kamikaze pilots, but as much to note differences between the context of that war and present exigencies. Guernica (also cited) reminds us that the deliberate military targeting of entire towns by palpably monstrous regimes is also nothing new; it has in fact shadowed the entire twentieth century. Intelligence services have also played a seminal role in the use of covert killing devices in the post-war period, not just the terrorist organizations they fight.

Another key date to consider is January 1947, when Zionist guerrillas, the Stern Gang, drove a truck of explosives into a British police station in Haifa to lethal effect. Today the message is that virtually any urban space is vulnerable to a sufficiently resourceful agent armed with Semtex, or the like. Only the most restricted, so-called "Green Zones" of cities such as Baghdad can be made relatively impregnable. Passenger planes now tend to be well guarded, but, despite the millions poured into Pentagon research, the simplest device of all, explosives strapped to human bodies and carried into the midst of a crowd, remains terrifyingly unstoppable.

De Masi makes the point that assumptions about the identity and mental state of the people in question should not be made in advance. Stereotypes and preconceptions, he shows, unhelpfully clutter the terrain. I was reminded of the scene in Kathryn Bigelow's movie, *The Hurt Locker* (2008) where an apparent suicide bomber, replete with his deadly arsenal, is dramatically exposed to view. He stands alone, under the apprehensive gaze of soldiers and civilians in an open space. A bomb disposal expert, the equivocal hero of the story, approaches, only to realize the man is chained to the explosives, and has no wish to die, nor any key to escape his padlocks. A timer is ticking and there is a moment of strange and painful intimacy between the two men. The "terrorist" has been made to carry out the task and is in terror of his own death. It is too late, the officer flees, and the explosion goes off.

More typically, it seems, the bomber is not only a believer, but also believes himself or herself to have chosen this fate quite knowingly and willingly. At the same time, that will is usually nurtured and shepherded by others, the volunteer taken to the point of no return. Among the interesting aspects of this discussion is the description of the subject's training: the costly psychological passage towards the act. The price is the studied demolition of the will to live, or even to hesitate, but this is not to say the person is necessarily mad, or, at least, not in the way that psychiatry has traditionally defined madness.

The author does not let us forget the tragic and unjust political and historical circumstances in which such missions generally take place. Nor does he fail to observe shameful horrors and grotesque actions committed in our name. Manichean thinking, "us" *vs.* "them", is part of the splitting that requires psychoanalytical attention. Psychoanalysis is well placed to consider this terrain. Freud, after all, soon disabused his reader of the belief that the less palatable aspects of psychic life were the exclusive preserve of some aberrant sub-category of people. Indeed, while De Masi is a committed psychoanalyst, his work is not that of the one-track missionary. His approach, on the contrary, is a humane antidote to zealotry. In keeping with this spirit, he is mindful of the risk that psychoanalysis may claim too much and too fervently, not least in applying itself to politics. He approaches his theme as an open inquiry, acknowledging at the outset his own puzzlement. The book is like the record of a learning curve. Much of the first part defines the horizons of the problem, draws out the sources, an exercise in discovery rather than didactic instruction.

This is in keeping with psychoanalysis at its best, since the practice of the "talking cure" first began in the act of careful listening to, rather than talking at, people. Freud had his theories, but he was also interested in what the other had to say, adjusting his theories accordingly. He attended more closely than did his professional peers, to the drift of the patient's speech. One of the features of so much current representation of the suicide bomber is that it fills in gaps in knowledge with preconceptions, painting a picture of demons and fanatics, as though this is all that need be said, the end, rather than the beginning, of the story. By definition we are usually in the dark; the successful perpetrator leaves only messages (often chillingly depersonalized) in advance of the deed, not personal reflections on the consequences of the crime. The work of reflection, reconstruction and of mourning is largely left to others.

De Masi makes ample use of luminaries in his own field (notably Klein and Bion). But neither in this discussion nor in his earlier key work, does he merely parrot past masters. Their insights cannot provide a sufficient basis on which to consider the present political conjuncture. The author has his own distinctive, psychoanalytical voice, and he articulates well the possibilities, and limits, of applied Freudian thought. Thus, he introduces intriguing clinical vignettes into this discussion, but with some circumspection, asking whether they may—rather than insisting that they must—throw light on the core problems of the book.

The Enigma follows on, naturally, it could be said, from the themes of De Masi's earlier work, including two wide-ranging books that are already available in English translation: *Making Death Thinkable* (2004) and *Vulnerability to Psychosis* (2009). Although there is a link to that noteworthy 2004 clinical and theoretical study of the place of dying and death (and of the denial of death) in psychic life, he is not, I repeat, suggesting, that the present inquiry is simply an adjunct to his previous study of madness. Indeed, more strongly than that, it can be said that his central contention is that "suicide terrorism cannot be explained away by individual pathology". *The Enigma* invites us to be almost as much concerned with the elucidation of differences as it is with locating the common structures of feeling or the psycho-political affinities in different theatres of conflict. Hence, he reminds us of the "huge gulf [that] separates a Palestinian seeking the establishment of a nation, a Chechen demanding independence from Russia, a Bosnian compelled to fight in order to avoid annihilation by the Serbian army, a Tamil fighter claiming part of the territory occupied by government forces, and an al-Qaeda member who vows to destroy not only imperialism but also every form of Western culture". Moreover, as he notes, attitudes to life and death are themselves culturally and historically variable.

His argument for shifting the debate to the analysis of groups and organizations is persuasive. Just as the post-war human sciences had to expend considerable effort in showing that Nazism was not the work merely of a mad individual, Hitler, nor just the creation of a cabal of unscrupulous and abnormal fanatics, Hitler's "gang", it will not do to "explain" suicide bombers or their organizations in psychiatric terms. We need to be wary of reconstituting new versions of what Michel Foucault once called "Les Anormaux". There are cases (De Masi cites the Sarin gas attacks on the Tokyo subway) that might indeed be understood as the terrible work of psychotic people, but more commonly, there is a purposive logic (hateful and misguided though it may be). If, as Clausewitz once said, war is politics by other means, suicide bombing is merely a tool of that war, albeit a war that is not fought by traditional armies. Such missions endeavour to secure political leverage; they punish civilian populations in order to demoralize the perceived enemy, and/or make the costs of military occupations too high.

Historians and political scientists debate how much suicide missions in particular contexts have actually contributed to the achievement of the goals of the organizations that sponsor them. In some situations (granted a sufficient supply of suicidal volunteers, public pressure and other factors that sap the will of the occupier to remain), they have on occasion paid dividends. But even where the more powerful foe is not directly defeated, they serve as a bargaining chip in a potential negotiation: suicide missions can also be called off. They have made the price of military occupation, for instance in Lebanon, Iraq, Afghanistan, Chechnya (to name a few) higher than would otherwise be the case, although many times, they appear, more perversely, likely to thwart the very objectives that are claimed as the justification. What is involved, to borrow a phrase from an earlier period of terrorism, is a "strategy of tension". They ensure an escalation of violence and repression, and thus a radicalization and sharpening of the struggle between the two sides.

The column inches devoted to such stories, we all know, is inequitably spread. In the Stockholm case that dominated newspapers for a while, there was little, as it turned out, by way of carnage—the bomber's own death apart. It was the unexpected Scandinavian site and the possibility of high casualties (had all gone according to the design) that ensured prominent representation, especially in Europe. It turned out that further actions had been planned to take place soon after: an attempt in Copenhagen was foiled later in the same month. In the Stockholm case, Taimour Abdulwahab al-Abdaly, an Iraqi-born Swede detonated a car bomb before killing himself with a second device attached to his body. It seems he was heading for a shopping centre and—presumably inadvertently—set the bomb off prematurely.

According to emails sent to a Swedish news agency and the security police, the particular catalyst was the Swedish cartoonist, Lars Vilks' offensive 2007 drawing, published in a Swedish paper, of the Prophet Muhammad (a source of indignation to countless Muslims around the world, as was the similar furore over cartoons in Danish papers). The presence of Swedish soldiers in Afghanistan was also noted: "Now your children, daughters and sisters shall die like our brothers and sisters are dying", he warned. Yours and ours: death relayed to the other, in the knowledge that it is an act of repetition and of transfer. Psychoanalysts sometimes talk of words as missiles that are designed to get unconscious feelings through to the object; perhaps the offending cartoons can be experienced as an impingement in that way, but they also have triggered a terrifyingly clamorous response, in which actual weapons become (lethal) messages of retribution.

Franco De Masi also acknowledges the differences between the terror used by states (to retain absolute power) and by groups that seek to overthrow governments. Moreover, although he considers the idea that modern terrorism is so massive in scale and mass slaughter now used so indiscriminately that it could be placed "on a par with genocide (of the Jews, the Armenians, or specific ethnic groups in the recent conflicts in Rwanda or Bosnia)", he also notes that such a claim is questionable.

The architects of genocide do not aim, as do the architects of most terrorist outrages, to leave the target group in constant fear, but rather seek to wipe it out entirely. It was in fact in the context of Nazi policy that the Polish lawyer and émigré to the USA, Raphael Lemkin, coined the term "genocide" in 1943. The Jews were not (at least by the time of the Second World War) only to be terrorized and persecuted; it was not a question of splitting the adversary into live and dead parts, still less of seeking to "redeem" or convert those of a supposedly blasphemous faith. Rather, in that case, the aim was to achieve the entire eradication of the Jewish people. There is a difference, he writes, between killing off an entire people on one side, and weakening, frightening, and paralysing on the other. Where does the one slide into the other? Terrorism presupposes that a given population will both witness and suffer from a spectacular and unexpected act, or sequence of acts, of horror.

Finally, it should be stressed that *The Enigma of the Suicide Bomber* has many resonances in and for clinical work. Those descriptions, for instance, of the psychic trajectory of the "apprentice terrorist" who becomes "progressively isolated", "joins a new group" "undergoes comprehensive acculturation" leading to "a state of regressive dependence on the 'master' and the group itself", could serve as a powerful description of what happens sometimes in the psychoanalytic session, when any kind of "working group" between the analyst and patient, breaks down. Consider the following passage in that light:

To eliminate every affective link with the past, the aspiring suicide is given a new name, puts on new clothes, and is kept in isolation until the time of his mission. He must be rendered amorphous and devoid of personal history in order to become an undifferentiated cell in the social organism. To use a biological metaphor, the social group in this case behaves like a living body that uses antibodies and the cells of the immune system to defend itself and survive. It is these which neutralize and kill the alien elements that present a danger to the organism, dying themselves in the process. In this logic of enmity, suicide attackers correspond to the blood proteins or cells that specialize in self-sacrifice.

The author makes an important distinction between the explicit rage and suffering entailed in acts of aggression and a less obvious and more deadly form of destructiveness. Drawing on Freud's death drive and on Klein's object relations, he emphasizes the stealthy dissolution of bonds that may occur within. It is the nature of that *undoing* of the emotional tie that he is most concerned to highlight. De Masi calls this an "anti-relational process". Perhaps there is an analogy to be drawn between the silent movement of the suicide bomber inconspicuously through space (the mute Said finally taking his seat on the bus in *Paradise Now*) and the work of camouflaged auto-destruction that can proceed inside the psyche, and the analysis. Instead of loud internal protest or voluble pain, Said becomes still, remote and immovable (despite his friend's impassioned pleas), as far from the agent of a "crime of passion" as possible. De Masi imagines this as "the attainment of a special mental state in which feelings and emotions have been abolished". His reminder that aggression is not a synonym of destructiveness, but has its own properties, can usefully be applied in other situations as well.

If emotions, such as pity for the victims and for the dying self resurface, De Masi muses (with an eye still perhaps towards the denouement of *Paradise Now)* "the destructive action is blocked". "Every perverse system", he muses, "presents itself as a hyper-moral organization". A remark by Otto Kernberg (also cited here) is worth highlighting: "the understanding of fundamentalism, terrorism, and fanaticism may be powerfully enriched by psychoanalytic perspectives, and these current historical developments, in turn, may stimulate psychoanalytic development of the understanding of the expression of the unconscious in the social field". I commend this perturbing, challenging, and highly contemporary book: it is a far cry from the twenty-four-hour cycle of rolling news sound bites, a culture to which we become too easily inured.

Introduction

"What can be done in such a position? Keep strangling them more and more, keep mowing down hundreds of Palestinians in Gaza, most of whom are innocent civilians like us? . . . Go to the Palestinians, Mr Olmert, do not search all the time for reasons not to talk to them. . . . There is no time. Should you delay, in a short while we will look back with longing at the amateur Palestinian terror. We will hit our heads and yell at our failure to exercise all of our mental flexibility, all of the Israeli ingenuity to uproot our enemies from their self-entrapment"

(David Grossman, from a speech delivered on the anniversary of the death of Yitzhak Rabin, 4 November 2006)

The savagery that shook the world on 11 September 2001 has since become a virtual commonplace in our lives. The repeated viewing of slaughtered bodies plunging from the burning skyscrapers, the images of dozens of charred corpses in the aftermath of explosions and attacks, the imploring, desperate voices of hostages doomed to die, and the footage of severed heads on our television screens—all these have become instances of everyday madness to which we have paradoxically become habituated as if they were an unavoidable evil. In this book I shall address a particular aspect of terrorism, namely suicide terrorism, which is responsible for more deaths than any other form. Postulating that terrorism is fuelled by the hate that arises out of the desperate conditions in which some populations are forced to live, I shall explore the mental state that compels certain individuals to perform monstrous, inhuman acts. In my view, however, trauma alone does not fully account for the making of suicide attackers; in order for these to become an offensive weapon, there must also be a political entity that encourages and organizes them. If such entities are led by persons imbued with an omnipotent ideology, destructive hate will assume an overwhelming dimension that will brook no alternative.

Attempting to investigate the subjective state of mind of a suicide terrorist may appear an ambitious task, not only on account of the mystery surrounding any human being who takes his own life, but also because the exploration of any psychological manifestation must be based on personal emotional experiences on which it is possible to reflect.

In killing himself, a suicide terrorist takes the reasons for his act with him to the grave. The information sources available on the Internet or in specialized journals on the phenomenon of suicide terrorism—a subject that now also features in literature and film—have mushroomed over time. However, most of this information concerns the environmental, social, religious, political, or strategic aspects, and we are told little about the subjective experience of a particular individual who decides to become a human bomb.

Why does someone resolve to take his own life in order to murder other people? What is the state of mind in which he can commit such an act? Is the decision to sacrifice himself his own, or is he a sick, dehumanized robot at the mercy of unscrupulous groups? How can a person sever all bonds with his family and friends and with the country in which he was born and grew up?

Terrorism has always been a weapon of intimidation, available to a minority wishing to accomplish a political object, but with the appearance of human bombs its quality has changed almost beyond recognition—by virtue not only of its symbolic character but also of its effectiveness. Mass destruction can be regarded as a further escalation of the trend in warfare that began in the last century:

over time, terror has become one of the principal instruments of military strategy. Modern war, it seems, is increasingly character- ized by the aim of arousing terror in the civilian population even in cases of manifest disparity of the military forces in the field. Inducing panic in the civilian population through the destructive potential of the offensive weapons, such as nuclear bombs, avail- able to states has now become the specific objective of a belligerent nation and one of the means of resolving conflicts.

In the past, wars were fought between armies. Although civilian populations suffered hardship, devastation, and even reprisals, they were not the main target of hostile action. However, since Guernica, the strategy of terror has been applied without limitation or any humanitarian consideration by all governments that could permit themselves to do so. Lethal air raids have been specifically directed at defenceless populations in order to terrorize an entire nation and induce it to surrender. With the bombing of Dresden and other German cities, some of which were utterly razed to the ground, tens of thousands of women, children, and old people were killed, while the military, often garrisoned outside the big towns and cities, were spared.

The risk of indiscriminate slaughter of innocent civilians exists in any modern conflict. Indeed, public opinion welcomes with relief the declared intention of a military power to wage a "clean" war— that is, to employ "surgical means" in order to spare the civilian population. These aseptic operations then inflict "collateral dam- age" on civilian victims, cut down every day owing to human error.

However, over and above the indiscriminate use of acts of ter- ror to subdue the enemy, what is truly unprecedented and disturb- ing about contemporary terrorism is the *large-scale deployment of suicide attackers*—particularly as witnessed again and again in Iraq after the Anglo-American intervention. By virtue of the component of suicide, contemporary terrorism differs qualitatively—in human as well as political terms—from forms such as those seen in the past in Italy, Germany, or Ireland.

Suicide terrorism in the past

Instances of suicide terrorism have of course been recorded throughout the history of human populations. The most notorious cases were the Jewish *Sicarii* of the first century AD and the Shi'a Muslims of the twelfth and thirteenth centuries. The latter sect used hashish to prepare for their acts—hence our word *assassin*. The *Hashishiyun* also used assassination as an instrument of purification. The victims might perhaps be members or officials of the Sunni regime, who were executed in public as a demonstration of their responsibility. Having completed the assassination, the killer would often take his own life as an expression of the purity of his intentions and in order to be sure of entering Paradise.

Other examples of violence perpetrated by suicide attackers occurred between the eighteenth and early twentieth centuries during the course of European expansion on the Malabar Coast (present-day Kerala, in south-west India), Sumatra, and the southern Philippines. The Malabar suicide attacks were directed initially against the Portuguese and subsequently against the British, in reprisal for the brutal repression of the native population. In Sumatra, the Dutch occupiers were devastated by such attacks (120 recorded cases). In the southern Philippines, the victims were the Spanish conquerors, who forced the local Muslims to convert to Catholicism. The attackers were known as *juramentados*—that is, persons who had sworn to kill as many people as possible before they died (Seidensticker, 2006).

The kamikaze pilots deployed by the Japanese armed forces in the latter part of the Second World War are a case apart (the Japanese air force alone is thought to have undertaken 4000 kamikaze missions). However, these were military personnel trained to confront death in battle, and their targets were other military personnel.

This limitation has ceased to exist in our time, and with it the distinction between military and civilian targets. Furthermore, today's suicide terrorist may equally well be a woman.

Absence of anxiety

Many Western observers have emphasized the link between suicide terrorism and a certain type of Islamic faith with powerful irrational and violent components. Although the relationship between the individual and society and the concept of individual death are admittedly different in non-Western traditions, analysis of the phenomenon of suicide terrorism cannot be confined to the social context or to a people's historical heritage.

Human beings have powerful innate defences against the danger of death, and it is impossible to bring about one's own destruction calmly and without anxiety. Our biologically given will to survive stubbornly opposes the event of death. Anxiety about our end bears witness to the persistence within our internal world of forces that cause us to value and defend life.

According to media reports and video testaments issued before their deaths, however, the young suicides-to-be appear calm, serene, and utterly undisturbed by the thought of their own demise.

In the riskiest missions of the past, attackers could, in extremis, seek a possible life-saving solution. In contemporary terrorism, on the other hand, suicide is inevitable. The attacker knows that only the sacrifice of his life will enable him to complete his mission—that is, to inflict maximum destruction and death on the enemy.

How then does the terrorist mentality, or at least that of certain groups, differ from its earlier incarnations? What has changed so radically that one of the most powerful human anxieties, the one that is automatically unleashed by the danger of death, is overcome in the service of the aggressive purpose? What has enfeebled the taboo on suicide so prominent in every religious creed to the point that an attacker is prepared to lay down his life in order to strike a blow at the enemy?

As a student of death anxiety and the defences universally erected against it, I have a particular interest in this problem. In my book *Making Death Thinkable* (De Masi, 2002), I attempted to describe the anguish that assails us all in accepting the idea of our end. This event can arouse violent anxiety in every human being, resulting in a heavy burden of anxiety throughout life. Reflection on our transience is a complex and difficult process, and the older we grow, the less we can ignore the fact that our lives have a natural limit.

A mass pathology?

In other words, the fear of death, to which nature seems to have entrusted the task of protecting life, can by no means be avoided. Where death anxiety is not aroused by the danger of losing one's life, psychopathology is usually involved. Does this account for suicide terrorism?

In attempting to understand this senseless, unthinkable behaviour, one inevitably thinks of patients, such as anorexics, drug addicts, borderlines, or psychotics, whose pathological actions are seemingly directed towards their own annihilation. In these cases too, death anxiety disappears, in favour of an inexplicable attraction to destruction of the self. Suicide attackers may perhaps exhibit a comparable form of psychopathology.

The Japanese kamikaze pilots believed that the Emperor was a god and were prepared to die for him on account of this conviction. They thought that after death their soul would go to the shrine of Yasukuni, where it would then repose in peace. Such a belief, which is similar to the motivation of certain Islamic terrorists who expect to gain immediate access to Paradise when they die, is analogous in some respects to certain severe pathological states. A schizophrenic who plunges from the top of a tall building does not think he will thereby meet his end, but imagines that he will fly. Similarly, an anorexic patient is unaware that she will die, but instead believes that she will soon be transformed into pure spirit.

However, a specific psychopathology cannot readily be discerned in the individuals concerned; nor is there such a thing as a typical suicide terrorist. Each attacker differs in age, sex, family status, culture, and even religion; the political or ideological groups to which terrorists belong are extremely diverse.

Psychoanalytic-type studies seeking to identify specific unconscious structures in suicide terrorists (for instance, an excessive split between ideal aspects of the self, or projection of the bad on to the enemy due to early infantile traumas) have also not proved useful in solving the problem. After all, some suicide attackers had undisturbed, protected childhoods.

Every attempt to typify the phenomenon in terms of psychopathology has failed owing to the diversity and complexity of the situations concerned. Even if the most detailed biographies or exhaustive personal communications were available, the attackers' histories and motivations would not be mutually comparable and could not be fitted into any nosographic classification.

The common elements in suicide terrorism should perhaps be sought not so much in the individuals concerned as in the dynamics rooted in the group or family history. Our attention should be focused on group rather than individual pathologies. It may be the *extreme situations experienced by the group*—situations that are either objectively extreme or perceived as such—that give rise to *paradoxical behaviour* at individual level.

The fundamental characteristic of the phenomenon of suicide terrorism is that the group no longer performs the function of safeguarding the lives of individuals when it authorizes certain members to sacrifice themselves in order to destroy the enemy. Given what is seen as a lethal danger, the *social contract*, which protects individual lives and maintains the bond between the individual and the group, ceases to apply.

A similar situation is also implicit in war: here again, the protection of individual group members' lives is suspended for the sake of defending the community. As specialists in war, those members are asked to lay down their lives in combat if necessary. In traditional wars, however, the risk of loss of life is shared by the community as a whole, and death is an event that is possible but not certain from the outset.

In the case of suicide terrorism, the sacrifice of the attacker's life is inevitable. A prey to unceasing despair, the community undertakes defensive acts whose effect is to perpetuate the trauma rather than to modify it. The terrorist becomes the agent of the group's basic assumption and is incorporated into the sadomasochistic fabric that characterizes his community. In this situation, the aim is not to defeat the enemy on the field of battle, but to wound and traumatize him.

Self-annihilation

In these *extreme situations*, certain members of the group are called upon to give up their individuality even before they end their lives. Prior to his self-immolation, a terrorist must abolish the emotions that underpin his personal identity and immerse himself completely in the group mentality. This process is probably easier in communities where the dialectic between the individual and society is less pronounced.

Traumas affecting the community—for instance, wars—first of all upset the balance between the need to safeguard the group on the one hand and individual liberty on the other. Whereas the value of individuality is thoroughly accepted and undisputed in the West, values that reinforce group homogeneity to the detriment of the individual hold sway in other contemporary societies. It is in the latter that the individual can more readily be asked, at times of crisis, to surrender his already weak identity in favour of collective needs. As an act of simultaneous defence and aggression, the affected society organizes itself in ideological structures that suspend the space of personal existence, even to the point of explicitly calling on some of its members to sacrifice their lives.

In some particularly traumatized communities, or ones with highly ideologized leaders, suicide martyrdom is exalted as a weapon necessary for the defence of a population that lacks an appropriate offensive capability. The victim, used as a weapon, must first relinquish his character as a person. This aim is achieved by psychological techniques directed towards abolishing the sense of identity, to which the future human bombs are sometimes but not always exposed. To eliminate every affective link with the past, the aspiring suicide is given a new name, puts on new clothes, and is kept in isolation until the time of his mission. He must be rendered amorphous and devoid of personal history in order to become an undifferentiated cell in the social organism. To use a biological metaphor, the social group in this case behaves like a living body that uses antibodies and the cells of the immune system to defend itself and survive. It is these which neutralize and kill the alien elements that present a danger to the organism, dying themselves in the process. In this logic of enmity, suicide attackers correspond to the blood proteins or cells that specialize in self-sacrifice.

The biological metaphor aside, it is not easy to understand how the psychological and biological forces that sustain individuality and the survival of the individual can be inactivated so that the individual can sacrifice himself, seemingly without conflict, for the sake of the social organism's survival.

Collective trauma

My contention in this volume is that suicide terrorism cannot be linked to any individual pathology. The phenomenon is unique and must be investigated in its specificity. In the first part of the book, I present a general picture of suicide terrorism, reviewing the opinions and contributions of some of the authors who have studied the subject. These chapters are predominantly historical and sociological in character, and serve as an introduction to the subsequent psychodynamic consideration. I was concerned to reconstruct the origins of the phenomenon and to describe its quantitative and organizational aspects, before embarking on an analysis of the more individual and subjective components. The second part comprises an in-depth examination of the psychological and emotional world of those who are seduced by the suicidal project, and an attempt to identify its underlying self-destructive motivation from the psychoanalytic point of view.

In writing this book, I drew on a large number of information sources, including valuable data on suicide terrorism from the World Wide Web. It is unfortunate that these contributions, composed for specialized journals or international organizations, cannot be more widely disseminated, because they facilitate understanding of a highly complex phenomenon. These texts tell the stories of certain men and women who sacrificed their lives in order to kill others. They show that it is only by placing the lives of those who have perpetrated such horrendous crimes in their emotional, social, and family context that we can comprehend how such an act can be committed by a human being and not by a monster.

To illustrate the novelty and specificity of the phenomenon, I have tried to distinguish the behaviour of a suicidal martyr from seemingly analogous manifestations such as martyrdom, murder-suicide, sadomasochistic relationships, or other forms of individual pathology. I would emphasize that, whereas a suicidal terrorist attack can be described as a crime against humanity, its protagonists cannot be classified as criminal or insane.

One of the possible approaches to understanding the reasons for this new kind of barbarity is to see it as symptomatic of a total lack of empathy and sympathy with the suffering of peoples with different traditions, histories, and trends, which have become embroiled in radical conflict with each other. Our world today seems incapable of desisting from devastating acts that trigger mourning on a vast scale, which will inevitably perpetuate equally violent and destructive responses. As many authors have indicated, what fuels the vocation to suicidal martyrdom is ongoing trauma and contempt for the dignity of entire communities. For this reason, the central part of this book is devoted to emotional trauma and its developments in both the individual and society.

However, not everything can be accounted for by the traumatic situation of certain populations condemned to live in despair. The evidence does not suggest that the phenomenon of global terrorism always has a traumatic origin. The leaders of international terrorism are not poor individuals weighed down by years of persecution and injustice, but possess immense wealth, are familiar with the mechanisms of international finance, and sometimes operate within the very capitalist organizations they have vowed to destroy.

In this volume I contrast this type of terrorism, which employs highly refined strategies and has vast operational resources at its disposal, with national terrorism characterized by clear-cut political aims. International terrorism is not occasioned by a traumatic wound, but is organized by a political and religious elite that is accustomed to dominate and fears the elimination of its ideology or the erosion of its power. This elite has the technological competence, coupled with an array of sophisticated facilities, to strike at the critical infrastructure of its enemy, with whose strengths and possible weaknesses it is familiar.

In the search for analogies from the past, not only many similarities but also significant differences emerge between the various suicidal martyrs. The Japanese kamikaze, for example, were military personnel trained to defy death. By virtue of the cult of the Emperor and of military honour, together with contempt for their own lives, these carefully selected men did not for an instant hesitate to act when ordered to transform themselves into human bombs.

The situation of a suicidal martyr is different: he is a mere non-violent civilian, who has never borne arms and does not know how to use explosives. His death wish arises spontaneously. If it were only coercion or indoctrination that compelled him to lay down his life, the instinct to survive might emerge at the last minute and cause him to desist from his act. The self-annihilation of the terrorist calls for the sharing of an extreme and tragic vision of political struggle. It is the political aim that motivates the suicidal martyr's act and makes his position very different from that of a soldier.

I shall attempt in this book to unravel the tangled web of emotions that have found no other means of expression than that of violent, vengeful action.

Notes

1. Translator's note: For convenience, the masculine form is used where applicable for both sexes throughout this translation.
2. Ivan Morris (1975, p. 316) quotes a poem by a Japanese kamikaze pilot who died in Okinawa in 1945: "[Soon] I shall vanish for good. I shall quietly become nonexistent, like a nameless star that fades away at dawn".

CHAPTER ONE

A strategic aim

"The war of absolute enmity knows no bracketing. The
constant fulfillment of absolute enmity provides its own
meaning and justification"

(Schmitt, 2007)

Problems of definition

The word *terror* is of Latin origin and the concept refers to the
sensation of unmitigated fear and anxiety that is unleashed
by sudden confrontation with death. One of the presupposi-
tions of terrorism is that individuals will be prepared to sacrifice
their autonomy and independence for the sake of escaping from
this fear. Arousing panic is indeed a way of securing the enslave-
ment of another person. Submerging the other in death anxiety is
the aim of terrorism, a form of violence directed towards the generation of fear. The object of this violence is to bend the victim to the
terrorist's will.

However, a definition that emphasizes the effect of fear on
human beings is not an adequate political description of terrorism.

Furthermore, present-day terrorism shows a different face from that of the past, owing to the destructive potential of modern weapons, and because the aims and the political instigators of terrorism are not the same. For this reason, it is difficult to give an unambiguous definition of the phenomenon of terrorism, which, as certain authors (e.g., Twemlow & Sacco, 2002) point out, is in fact influenced by the social and political values of the time.

At international level, too, it has not been possible to reach agreement on the definition of terrorism. The question had already arisen at the Munich Olympics of 1972, when a group of Palestinians abducted nine Israeli athletes. The United States' draft resolution condemning terrorism was rejected by the non-aligned countries, which maintained that the struggle for national liberation was legitimate and instead condemned "repressive and terrorist acts by colonial, racist and alien regimes" (Haffey, 1998, p. 1). In spite of many attempts, the United Nations has been unable to arrive at a consensus on the definition of terrorism, precisely because of the irreconcilable disagreement between those member states (the Arab nations) that want to include, within such a definition, the concept of state terrorism, and others—the United States and Israel in particular—that cannot accept its inclusion.

A definition put to the United Nations General Assembly is as follows:

> Any . . . act intended to cause death or serious bodily injury to a civilian, or to any other person not taking an active part in the hostilities in a situation of armed conflict, when the purpose of such act, by its nature or context, is to intimidate a population, or to compel a government or an international organization to do or to abstain from doing any act. [Article 2(b) of the International Convention for the Suppression of the Financing of Terrorism, 5 May 2004][1]

The disunity and scope for discretion on this issue are also illustrated by the differences between individual Western nations' views of Hezbollah ("the Party of God"), which is seen as a terrorist organization by the USA, the UK, and Israel, but not by other European states.

The assassinated former Prime Minister of Pakistan, Benazir Bhutto, described the dangers of these opposing positions, which represent different conceptions of political struggle, as follows:

Unless there is an agreement that terrorism knows no religion and no civilization, we could be on the precipice of a much more dangerous world. . . . Without a shared security mechanism and a definition of terrorism, the world could actually find itself in a holy war between Islam and the West. It's a war that no one wants—except the extremists. [Bhutto, 2002, after Vedantam, 2003]

State terrorism?

To understand the nature and objectives of terrorism, it must first be distinguished from other, apparently similar phenomena. For example, some commentators consider terrorism to be an appropriate description of the incursions by Israeli tanks into the Palestinian territories and refugee camps, a response deemed as violent and destructive as a human bomb. Does an indiscriminate counter-terrorist response constitute terrorism? Is state terrorism equivalent to that perpetrated by someone who uses bombs to induce panic and to upset a balance of power? It was Robespierre who, in the name of the ethical state, first justified state terrorism and claimed moral acceptability for the assassination of political enemies. Since the French Revolution, other states—for instance, those with National Socialist or communist regimes—have based their political activity on terror, whether for the sake of ideology, the morality of the nation, or class interests.

Terror perpetrated by the state can be distinguished from terrorism proper according to the differences in the respective ways of achieving, maintaining, or extending power. In state terrorism, violence is perpetrated against ethnic or other groups within a nation itself in order to render already existing political power absolute. In this case, the actions of the governing party need not, at least to a certain extent, be supported by the population. It is the state that organizes genocide, while at the same time denying it and concealing the evidence of massacres. In terrorism proper, on the other hand, violence directed towards the imposition of political change or the seizure of power is explicit and even extolled.

Terrorism must also be distinguished from the actions of insurgent groups fighting to subvert the government of a given state. Not only the political motivations of the terrorists, but also those of their political adversaries who define them as such, must be subjected to rigorous examination. After all, debatable and politically expedient use can be made of the term terrorism, for example when those prepared to use violence in fighting for a political cause are described as terrorists. Russia has defined the Chechen separatists as terrorists, China has done the same with the Uighurs, and India with the Kashmir separatists. In this connection, Vedantam (2003) invokes the *Rashomon effect*—a reference to Akira Kurosawa's eponymous film, which tells the story of one and the same crime from contrasting and irreconcilable viewpoints.

Akhtar (in Hough, 2004, p. 814) distinguishes two types of terrorism: *terrorism from above*, used by government forces to intimidate, persecute, and destroy minorities; and *terrorism from below*, which acts against the state with destructive means. For the National Research Council (2002, p. 29), terrorism is "a strategy of the weak against the strong". Both of these conceptions seem reductive against the background of the planet-wide dimension assumed by the phenomenon with the attack on New York's Twin Towers.

What then are the salient differences between contemporary terrorism—described by Bettini (2003) as *hyperterrorism*—and that of the past?

Terrorism and genocide

Terrorism has traditionally been used by political minorities wishing to undermine a hated authoritarian regime. From the anarchic regicides of the eighteenth century to the anti-Tsarist conspiracies, history is replete with homicidal acts intended to cause terror and chaos. The aim was to attack and destroy the symbol of power: with a single pistol shot, the anarchist would kill the sovereign and obliterate his charismatic image, with a view to destabilizing the entire tyrannical order.

Later, even democratic regimes were affected by the phenomenon; examples are the wave of bloody slaughter experienced in Italy in the 1970s, and Basque, Irish, or Chechen terrorism. In these cases, the terrorist attacks were not merely military actions, but were principally aimed at drawing the national or international community's attention to the relevant group's struggle. Coverage in the international media would ensure that the acts were seen as duly spectacular. As Benjamin Netanyahu, Prime Minister of Israel at the time of writing, rightly pointed out some years ago, without media coverage acts of terrorism would resemble the proverbial tree that falls silently in the forest.

The face of terrorism has changed in recent years. Mass slaughter, already a feature of the Algerian struggle for independence, or of the "strategy of tension" in Italy, is now employed so systematically that it has virtually become a strategy in itself. Its massive scale admittedly places terrorism on a par with genocide (of the Jews, the Armenians, or specific ethnic groups in the recent conflicts in Rwanda or Bosnia); however, the difference is that genocide is an action planned by the state with the aim of exterminating an ethnic group deemed to be hostile or different, whereas even large-scale terrorism is manifestly not directed towards extermination of the enemy. Its purpose is to strike indiscriminately, to arouse anxiety, and to confuse and disorientate the target group. The action must be spectacular in order to give rise to panic, and the destruction must be unpredictable, so as to weaken the enemy psychologically and to paralyse him.[2]

However, this aim is achieved only in the immediate aftermath of the attack. Once the panic is over, the target population defends itself and mobilizes in order to neutralize the danger.

In the case of genocide, on the other hand, examination of the victims' emotional reaction reveals the surprising fact of their passivity. Systematic violence by the state (state terrorism) gives rise to a mental condition that inhibits any reaction. From the extermination of the Armenians in Turkey to the genocidal policy of Stalin in the Soviet Union, from the destruction of the Jews in Europe to the massacres perpetrated by Pol Pot in Cambodia, "ethnic cleansing" in Bosnia, and the extermination of the Tutsi community in Rwanda, millions of people have been systematically slaughtered without any evidence of resistance. Genocide can be carried out, and terror can spread, because the persecuted community represents a minority within a state, lacks political control of the armed forces, and is therefore unable to defend itself.

The aim of terrorism is predominantly political. It seeks to provoke utterly indiscriminate reprisals, so as to compel the enemy to radicalize its own position and to generalize repression. In this way alone can more and more people be induced to see violence as the only possible way forward. Terrorism is intended precisely to divide and to arouse conflicting emotions. Its victims fear and hate it, but at the same time there are others who, while not sympathizing with it, consider it justified. According to certain strands of public opinion, its reasons are comprehensible, and they defend it as a possible instrument of struggle. Some years ago, the Egyptian writer Naguib Mahfuz, a winner of the Nobel prize for literature, stated in an interview with the *New York Times* that he disapproved of suicide attackers, but added that he could understand them.

To understand the specificity of the terrorist strategy, it is essential to bear in mind that its aim is to provoke the enemy and heighten the level of conflict. Considered in these terms, the psychology of terrorism is much more sophisticated and complex than repressive terror exercised by the state. Furthermore, terrorism relies on this blindness for its success.

The rationality of terrorism

Terrorism exists in different forms according to its immediate purpose. Robert Pape (2003) distinguishes three types on the basis of their short-term objectives.

The first is *demonstrative terrorism*, whose aim is principally to gain publicity, to recruit more activists, and to force the government to make concessions. Examples are the terrorist groups in Northern Ireland, or the Extraparliamentary Left in Italy. Their action takes the specific forms of hostage-taking, aggression against individual politicians, or bomb blasts of which prior warning is usually given.

The second type is *destructive terrorism*, which is more directly aggressive in nature and seeks to inflict losses on its opponents by killing their leaders. Examples are the Baader-Meinhof gang, the Irish Republican Army (IRA), and the Revolutionary Armed Forces of Colombia (FARC). The most successful group in the recent past was surely the now defeated Tamil Tigers, who assassinated the Indian Prime Minister Rajiv Gandhi in Madras in 1991 with the aid of a young female suicide bomber.

Thirdly, there is *suicide terrorism*, in which the suicide-to-be bears his cargo of death with a view to maximizing the damage caused. A broader definition of a suicide terrorist will include not only those who kill themselves in order to kill others, but also those who expect to lose their lives during the course of an attack. Baruch Goldstein is an example of the latter. Before embarking on his mission, he left a note for his family stating that he did not expect to return. He did indeed then die while killing a group of Palestinians in Hebron in February 1994. This second and less frequent type of suicide terrorist is not linked to any organization. The psychological dynamics underlying their acts are also very different from those of suicide terrorists belonging to organizations with a hierarchical structure, who sacrifice their lives for a political purpose.

Considered in these terms, suicide terrorism proper is not the fruit of irrational impulses or fanatical hatred (although certain aspects of these are never lacking), but pursues strategic objectives.

Pape (2003) shows that this was the situation in Lebanon and the Gaza Strip, as well as in Sri Lanka, where the Liberation Tigers of Tamil Eelam (LTTE) recruited members from the Hindu population and had a Marxist-Leninist ideology.

Even though many suicide terrorists may, at first sight, appear irrational or fanatical, this is not true of the political aims of their leaders. Nor has the policy of suicide terrorism failed to achieve results: in Lebanon, the Franco-American forces withdrew in 1983; Israel was compelled to pull out of that country in 1985 and of the Gaza Strip in 1994–1995; while Sri Lankan government forces withdrew from certain parts of the country in 1990.

According to the same author, who possesses one of the largest databases on suicide attacks, these results were not solely attributable to terrorist action, which, however, was certainly a factor in their achievement. He concludes that almost all suicide attacks are not motivated by religious fanaticism, but form part of a deliberate strategy of compelling states to withdraw troops from territories held to be illegally occupied. In other words, according to Pape, suicide terrorism is not irrational, as some earlier commentators (Kramer, 1990; Merari, 1990; Post, 1984) believed, but is an extreme form of what Thomas Schelling (1966) called the "rationality of irrationality".

Ideological terrorism

The matter is, in fact, probably not as straightforward as Pape's description suggests. There may be a difference between terrorism directed towards the achievement of an explicit goal (as perhaps with Lebanese or Palestinian terrorism) and another form that is more radical and destructive, has no demands, and has no wish to negotiate. The latter type (which includes the 11 September attacks) has its origins in the totalitarian ideology of *jihad* or the *al-Qaeda* organization, lacks a precisely defined objective, but presupposes an implacable ideological struggle waged without quarter.

The three forms of terrorism enumerated by Pape must therefore be supplemented by a fourth—namely, *international ideological terrorism*, the most dangerous type of all. Ideological terrorism is not confined to a specific geographical area—and therefore does not correspond to a state or a nation—but is *supranational* in character. Its aim is to create a war mentality so as to provoke acts of retaliation at international level, thus triggering a bloody global conflict.

From this point of view, the ideological fanaticism of its leaders is not attributable to the madness of an individual or group, but is in fact the expression of the lucid aim of imposing power by means of a planet-wide bloodbath. For this reason, whereas the main aim of traditional terrorism was to secure political concessions, since 11 September the message of international ideological terrorism has been that of all-out war. Given this aim, it is misleading and dangerous to respond to ideological terrorist attacks with a war mentality.

Our age has witnessed unprecedented manifestations of hostility between peoples. As Vedantam (2003) points out, during the period of the Cold War when the policy of terror was dictated by the nuclear stand-off, the confrontation between the two sides paradoxically involved certain aspects of mutual trust. Each could predict the other's moves and both wished to avoid destruction.

In the case of global Islamic terrorism, on the other hand, the enemy's moves and the resulting possible damage are unpredictable. Again, it is difficult to mount a credible threat to profoundly radical groups which act in secret and lack a centralized organization.

Since 9/11, the name of *al-Qaeda* has often been used in political declarations or after abductions or attacks as a label in order to arouse panic. However, many experts believe that the nucleus of this organization sustained a serious blow with the invasion of Afghanistan. But since then, a worldwide, supranational, social movement has developed, carried forward by many young people who have espoused the basic ideas of Osama bin Laden.

Whether or not a central command or a hierarchical organization of terrorism exists, the real problem is that the seed of global terrorism, having been allowed to thrive for some years, has borne fruit at world level.

In this book, I distinguish between *nationalist-type terrorism* and *global Islamic terrorism*. These two forms are commonly equated with each other, not only because the terrorist mentality has become a widespread mental habit, but also because both movements use suicide martyrs. In my view, however, they can be told apart by the political aims, motivations, careers, and *psychodynamics* of their respective suicide martyrs.

A highly economical weapon

The use of suicide terrorists presents many tactical advantages. Unlike the situation in an ordinary attack, in which several people operate in a group and hope to emerge unscathed, a suicidal martyr acts alone and is, by definition, not concerned for his own life; furthermore, he does not need complex training, and, since he is going to die, there is no risk that he will ever disclose the names of the attack organizers. In tactical terms, a suicide terrorist is a very intelligent weapon, even capable of taking autonomous decisions so as to maximize the destruction caused. Since he does not need to arrange an escape route, he is more dangerous than an ordinary terrorist, who hopes to stay alive in addition to striking at his target.

The organization itself, which cannot afford the luxury of losing skilled militants, can sacrifice human bombs who are unfamiliar with its structure and lack technological skills. By deliberately disobeying the rules that limit destructiveness, suicide terrorism raises the level of violence exponentially.

The preparation of a suicide attack is known to cost very little in relation to its outcome. All that is needed is a relatively small quantity of explosive, a battery, a switch and a length of wire, a little mercury and acetone, and a fabric belt. The most expense is incurred in transporting the terrorist to the attack site. The total cost in Palestine has apparently never exceeded two thousand dollars. The terrorist organization compensates the suicide's family with some $3500.

The first Palestinian suicide terrorist blew himself up in the West Bank in April 1993 (this information is taken from Hassan, 2001). In just a few years, from 1993 to 1998, there were thirty-seven human bombs, responsibility for twenty-four of the attacks being claimed by Hamas and thirteen by Islamic Jihad. Another twenty-six suicide terrorists perished during the second Intifada, which began in September 2000. Of these attacks, Hamas claimed responsibility for nineteen and Islamic Jihad seven. Some 215 Israelis were killed and 800 wounded. The attacks took place in shops, on buses, on street corners, and in cafés—wherever people meet.

Yahya Ayyash, an engineering student from the West Bank, was the first to suggest that Hamas should use human bombs in its military operations. In a letter to its leadership, he recommended the use of suicide attacks as one of the most effective means of inflicting decisive damage on the Israeli occupation forces. He wrote, "We paid a high price when we used only slingshots and stones. We need to exert more pressure, make the cost of the occupation that much more expensive in human lives, that much more unbearable" (Hassan, 2001). The assassination of Ayyash by the Israeli security forces in January 1996 set off a wave of suicide attacks.

Fathi Shiqaqi, the founder of the Palestinian Islamic Jihad, who was assassinated by Mossad, the Israeli secret service, in 1995, helped to provide a religious context for martyrdom, in a document setting out guidelines for suicide operations. It counters religious objections to the practice of suicide, which had begun a few years earlier in Lebanon. Shiqaqi encouraged the practice of *exceptional martyrdom*, which he exalted as a necessary tactic for the accomplishment of the cause of Allah:

> We cannot achieve the goal of these operations if our *mujahid* [holy warrior] is not able to create an explosion within seconds and is unable to prevent the enemy from blocking the operation. All these results can be achieved through the explosion, which forces the *mujahid* not to waver, not to escape; to execute a successful opera-

tion for religion and jihad; and to destroy the morale of the enemy and plant terror into the people. [*ibid.*]

He describes this capability as "a gift from Allah" (*ibid.*).

The greatest success, in terms of relative numbers of victims and attackers, was achieved on 11 September through the onslaught on New York's Twin Towers. How, unless they had condemned themselves to die, could nineteen attackers wreak such devastation and kill so many victims? When the planes were taken over, the passengers could not know that the hijackers were resolved to destroy themselves together with the machines, and they remained ignorant of the outcome of the mission until the end.

It has been calculated (Pape, 2003) that the 188 suicide terrorists who died between 1988 and 2001 killed an average of thirteen people each, not counting the victims of 9/11. The remaining 4155 terrorist incidents recorded worldwide during the same period resulted in an average of less than one death each (the total number of people killed was 3207). Suicide attacks in the period 1983 to 2001 amounted to 3% of all terrorist attacks, but accounted for 48% of total terrorism deaths (figures from the United States Department of State).

Some years ago (according to Schweitzer, 2001), the number of suicide attacks perpetrated in fourteen countries by seventeen terrorist organizations had already reached 300. Diego Gambetta (2005) gives a global figure of 500 attacks between 1981 and 2004, organized by thirty religious and political groups. Given the daily slaughter in Iraq, Afghanistan, and Pakistan, the number of victims is still (in 2010) growing at a vertiginous pace.

CHAPTER TWO

Psychoanalytic contributions

"There's no worse cataclysm than humiliation. It's an evil beyond measure, Doctor. It takes away your taste for life. And until you die, you have only one idea in your head: How can I come to a worthy end after having lived *miserable, and blind, and naked*?"

(Khadra, 2006)

Although the phenomenon of global terrorism is relatively recent, there has been no lack of psychoanalytic contributions on the subject. Some of them, published in American psychoanalytic journals, were composed more or less instantly after 9/11 by analysts who had in some cases actually been present as events unfolded. It is also worth recalling the solidarity displayed by the New York psychoanalysts who responded to the their city's drama by voluntarily offering counselling and listening services to the trauma victims.

Among the many papers published in the last few years, I shall mention just a small number that seemed to me most relevant to a consideration of the phenomenon of suicide terrorism.

13

Ruth Stein's (2002) paper "Evil as love and as liberation", published in *Psychoanalytic Dialogues* barely a year after the attack on the World Trade Center, is to my mind particularly interesting. The author attempts, in my view successfully, to analyse the mental state of a suicide killer inspired by religious fanaticism. She contends that total concentration on the vision of God, achieved by constant prayer and reading of religious texts, can result in a depersonalized trance state, a restriction of consciousness that enables terrorists to function competently in a mood of euphoria. At psychodynamic level, the idealized father–son bond transforms destructiveness into the ecstatic love of God. By virtue of this idealized fusion, terrorists come to believe that their act is nothing other than the fulfilment of the divine will.

Another significant contribution to the subject is the volume *Violence or Dialogue?* (Varvin & Volkan, 2003). One of the questions addressed by the authors, who come from nations with diverse religious traditions (Christianity, Judaism, Islam, and Hinduism), concerns possible psychoanalytic approaches to the understanding of terrorism and, given that terrorist acts are committed in the name of particular groups, the nature of the relationship between individual and collective psychology, the collective aspect being religious, ethnic, or ideological. Another issue considered is the generalized fear aroused at global level by terrorist acts.

The book is divided into three parts. The first concerns the role of religion, gender, and sociopolitical processes as substrates for terrorist acts; the second concentrates on the concepts of victimization, dehumanization, and generalized fear; and the third explores the mental processes that may be at work in the perpetrators.

Some selected contributions from this volume are summarized below in the belief that they will help to lay the foundations of a psychoanalytic consideration of terrorism in general and of suicide terrorism in particular.

As Volkan points out in his preface, the 11 September attackers, like so-called terrorists elsewhere in the world, are not monsters, but human beings engaged in inhuman acts. Psychoanalysis seeks to understand their motivation and to identify what it is in human nature that fuels such behaviour and the transformations that lead to the commission of such acts.

In his contribution, entitled "Terrorism and victimization: individual and large-group dynamics", Varvin (2003) attempts to identify the mental processes and dynamics of large groups involved in the phenomenon of terrorism. In his view, analysis of the irrational forces operating in the individual and the group suggests that the difference between state terrorism and that perpetrated by groups pursuing terror from below is less marked than is often assumed. The continuity between the two lies in the *terrorist mentality* that inspires both. Almost all religions have the potential for violence against other groups, and sometimes also within the group itself. The "holy war" of Christianity, the *"jihad"* of Islam, and the "just war" of Judaism are examples of wars legitimized by a religious creed. The "war on terror" is a recent example of a war justified by a religiously tinged politico-ideological discourse. The author maintains that violence leading to terrorism is generated by a threat to community cohesion and identity, resulting in the coincidence of personal and group identity. For Varvin, the experience of shame and of a narcissistic wound is the basic determinant of terrorism. When exposed to humiliation in a context of social violence, the individual tends to experience the narcissistic wound not only in the first person (since he is affected individually), but also as a member of the group to which he belongs. Revenge is legitimized by the need to restore the group's identity and honour. The author holds that the infliction of constant humiliation on a community makes for regression in both the individual and the group. However, in order for the terrorist mentality to become a political project, a strongly ideologized leadership must emerge.

In her contribution, "Hate, humiliation, and masculinity", Chodorow (2003) contends that poverty and illiteracy are not the decisive determinants of terrorism. After all, terrorists mostly have middle-class, privileged, or educated backgrounds. The principal factors in the development of a terrorist disposition are, in her view, feelings of hate and humiliation. The author wonders why, in the vast majority of cases, it is men who engage in terrorist violence. In her view, a basic characteristic of male identity manifested in particular circumstances—such as political or ethnic conflicts—is the conviction of *having to be* an adult man as opposed to being seen as a child. The adult male struggles in order not to appear inferior, humiliated, or ridiculous in the eyes of other men, whereas an equivalent attitude on the part of women is less in evidence. Terrorism is fuelled by a mixture of shame, humiliation, and narcissism. Collective violence and terrorism are often motivated by the memory of past defeats and humiliations, whether actual or presumed. As also observed in clinical practice, individuals who feel humiliated and mocked frequently react with rage and grandiosity. Women are less inclined than men to fight against difference, which is perceived as dangerous to personal identity. For this reason, in a political or ethnic conflict, identification with a powerful leader protects a man from humiliation, reinforcing the rejection of femininity and sexuality. If a man's sense of self really is more rigidly defensive than a woman's, it is understandable that women are less affected by threats to religious or political identity and hence less inclined to opt for terrorism.

In "Collective phantasms, destructiveness, and terrorism", Bohleber (2003) maintains that religious fanaticism is an important factor in rage and hate. In his view, the World Trade Center attackers were inspired by the need for religious salvation. The predominance of religious ideology does indeed clearly emerge from the instructions found in Mohammed Atta's luggage. Having offered his life to God and cleansed his heart of every negative feeling, the assassin is washed clean of any guilt: "Heaven is smiling, my young son, for you are marching into it" (Aust & Schnibben, 2002, p. 277). As to the role of religious ideology in terrorism, Bohleber holds that in the Islamic nations religion has taken the place of the nationalism which, in the West, has been the container for irrational and fantasy material. The link between narcissistic visions of purity and religious fanaticism is also of fundamental importance for an understanding of the cultural background to Islamic terrorism, in which the blend of fantasies of fusion and violence takes the concrete form of the search for martyrdom. The author discovers surprising analogies between contemporary terrorism and the warlike policies of National Socialism, which sent thousands of young Germans to their deaths with the words of Theodor Körner in their kitbags: "Happiness lies only in sacrificial death" (quoted in Margalit & Buruma, 2002). However, radical ideology alone does not make a suicide terrorist. This result is achieved only by special training and indoctrination, which can be administered in structures that immerse the trainee in a "parallel world" where the sense of personal identity is supplanted by complete identification with the aims of the group. A survivor from a training camp for suicide terrorists in Lebanon reported that, in his organization, young martyrs-to-be lived in ascetic conditions, under the constant supervision of an imam. They were divided into groups, from which a sacrificial victim was from time to time selected. The chosen one was required to put on a suicide vest and to blow himself up by driving a vehicle into a wall. All this was done before the eyes of his companions.

Even if the training demanded by global terrorist movements, such as Islamic Jihad, presupposes immersion in a parallel world with no possibility of return, that alone would not suffice without the personal crisis that impels some young men to make such a choice. (Documentary evidence shows that, in the case of Palestinian terrorism, many young men approach the organization as volunteers and carry out their mission without any specific form of training or indoctrination.) Bohleber mentions the case of Said Bahaji, a Moroccan who had lived with Mohammed Atta in Hamburg, where he had graduated with distinction. Having formed a relationship with a European girl, he had been forced to leave her on account of opposition from her parents. Following this emotional trauma, Said had cut himself off from people, embraced religion, and begun to associate with a group of Islamic extremists. He had then started distributing anti-Jewish Islamic libels, and joined the group that would eventually perpetrate the New York slaughter. After marrying a German Islamic woman and fathering a child with her, Said disappeared in August 2001.

In Akhtar's contribution, "Dehumanization: origins, manifestations, and remedies" (2003), the phenomenon of terrorism is seen as centred on the process of dehumanization, which involves the elimination of any emotional perception. The author postulates that we all have a latent tendency towards dehumanization, which can be activated in conditions of bio-psychosocial stress, humiliation, poverty, and absence of solidarity and understanding. Without a consideration of the context in which terrorism comes into being, the *war on terror* is not only a metaphorical absurdity, but also a recipe for ongoing bloodshed.

In "Traumatized societies", Volkan (2003) emphasizes the link between trauma and terrorism, and shows that, in the case of a trauma following an ethnic, national, or religious conflict, the affected group regresses and the development of community life is blocked. If circumstances do not allow the members of the group to make sense of their humiliation, to mourn for their losses, and to arrive at a response based on solidarity, the sense of victimization will pervade the entire community. In this author's view, traumatized adults deposit their experiences of anxiety into their children, and these experiences have a cumulative effect on the form and content of the identity of the group as a whole. This results in the formation of what he calls the *"chosen trauma"*, which may persist for years or even centuries. The task of subsequent generations will be to keep the memory of the humiliation alive and to avenge it.

Awad, who grew up in a Palestinian refugee camp in Beirut and trained as a psychoanalyst in Canada, where he now lives, has direct experience of the Islamic world. In his contribution, "The minds and perceptions of 'the others'" (2003), he attempts to speak in the name of the Islamic Arab group from which all the suicide attackers in the Middle East and the United States stem. He points out that the concept of a non-religious Arab identity is quite recent, having arisen at the beginning of the twentieth century and only in the Islamic nations of the Mediterranean. Having gained political power (for instance in Turkey or Egypt), nationalism is now progressively losing ground to Islamist movements. While the nationalists are modernists who have accepted many Western values, the majority of Islamists are anti-modernist and anti-democratic. However, neither political tendency has developed a sense of political democracy. The Islamists are *anti-democratic* by definition, because for them authority is personified by the religious hierarchy; the nationalists, on the other hand, are *undemocratic* for internal reasons, because they have not managed to create truly representative institutions. Neither of the two movements has succeeded in developing a system capable of sustaining economic growth, while at the same time many Western political choices and military interventions have exacerbated the situation, arousing rage and indignation among the Islamic populations. Since the perpetrators of the suicide attacks in the United States came from Arab nations not occupied by foreign forces, these manifestations are seen to be a violent reaction by an extremely conservative society afraid of being colonized by an alien power and Western values. For this reason, many Arabs and Muslims, although horrified by such suicide attacks and the deaths of so many innocent civilians, do not consider these crimes to be any more heinous than the slow, methodical killing of *their own* innocent fellow-citizens by the Western powers. Awad ultimately distinguishes between the *cold* hate of the West and the State of Israel, on the one hand, and the *hot* hate of the Palestinians, other Arabs, and Muslims, on the other. Cold hate sometimes proves more lethal than hot hate.

*   *   *

Another relevant text is the compilation of contributions to a symposium organized by the Milan Psychoanalysis Centre in May 2006, whose title translates as "The roots of hate: an analysis of the phenomenon of terrorism". At this meeting, papers were presented by Claudia Peregrini and Almatea Usuelli, two analysts from Milan involved in a study group on the phenomenon of terrorism; then a Palestinian analyst, George Awad, and an analyst from Israel, Emanuel Berman, put forward their respective points of view.

Terrorism is neither specific to our time nor an imported phenomenon, but in fact originated on our own European soil. This aspect is addressed in the contribution of Agnese Grieco, a theatre director and author of books on philosophy and literature, as well as a playwright whose works have been staged in Italy and Germany. She points out that violence and death are the taboos which the terrorist mind appropriates and whose liberating power it extols. This is an image of redeeming death, which, however, is at the same time robbed of the objective element of mourning. As officiants of death, terrorists avoid mourning.

The contributions of Claudia Peregrini and Almatea Usuelli are devoted to this now more or less widespread form of contemporary warfare, which seems to have replaced the fear of nuclear war that threatened mankind in previous decades. The papers presented by George Awad and Emanuel Berman are interesting for their differing standpoints, the latter being more intimate and deeply felt on the psychoanalytic level, while the emphasis of the former is more historical and political, opening a window on the traumatically tinged aggressive tendencies of a part of the Muslim world. The compilation ends with a contribution by Mario Pirani, the well known Italian essayist and journalist, who was also invited to take part.

I can report that the presentations gave rise to a vigorous debate with contributions from the floor, with members of the audience clearly emotionally involved and remaining until the end. This tells us that people expect psychoanalysis to help explain the senseless violence that has now reached levels intolerable to both the individual and society.

In a recent contribution in the *International Journal of Psychoanalysis*, the eminent figure of Otto Kernberg, a past president of the IPA, recommends a consideration of global terrorism, which may even broaden our psychoanalytic horizons. He writes:

> ... the understanding of fundamentalism, terrorism, and fanaticism may be powerfully enriched by psychoanalytic perspectives, and these current historical developments, in turn, may stimulate psychoanalytic development of the understanding of the expression of the unconscious in the social field. [Kernberg, 2006, p. 925]

It is important to bear in mind that the tendency to commit dehumanizing acts is in fact inherent in our nature, and that, given appropriate circumstances, such destructiveness can be triggered in any human being. In other words, it is not enough to see suicide terrorism as one of the barbaric phenomena of the contemporary world; it must also be recognized as a possible extreme, mistaken response to the evil of our time.

CHAPTER THREE

Origins and profile

"A suicide bomber in Palestinian society at one point was like a movie star. You achieved almost instant fame. Posters at your death. Martyr cards made on your behalf"

(Oliver & Steinberg, 2005)

S uicide terrorists have often been portrayed as disturbed individuals, cast out from the society in which they live, unable to behave autonomously and responsibly, and driven to kill for insane reasons and out of hate for Western civilization. Alternatively, suicide martyrs have been regarded as the product of a form of archaic thought—naïve individuals manipulated by unscrupulous political organizations.

Numerous studies of the terrorist personality have been published, but their conclusions are extremely divergent. They can be divided into two broad categories, *pathologizing* and *non-pathologizing*.

Pathologizing versions

The psychological profile of the suicide terrorist that emerges from the earlier contribution of Merari (1990) and from Post's 1990 paper is of a socially isolated individual, young and unmarried, and probably suffering from a mental abnormality. Merari, in particular, suggests that the cultural environment and religious context are irrelevant to the choice of suicide terrorism, and that the motivation in this case is no different from that of someone who takes his own life for personal reasons. The same author (Merari, 2002) later modified his position, even claiming that the phenomenon could be understood only if investigated on the level of the social organizations that fuelled it. Individual problems alone were no longer seen as an adequate explanation.

On the basis of the biographies of several terrorists, Post (1984) maintains that aggression, the constant search for excitation, and action-orientated behaviour are characteristics encountered in the personalities of those destined to become terrorists, who are often motivated by failure in their personal lives. A few years later, the same author (Post, 1990) contends that, although falling within the category of normality and not suffering from any clinically ascertainable mental disorder, terrorists will have sustained infantile traumas, and are more inclined to commit acts of violence precisely for that reason. Their defences are splitting of the personality and outward projection of aggressive conflicts; however, these manifestations can also be observed in sufferers from narcissistic disorders. For this reason, Post maintains that infantile wounds that have not been worked through impel these individuals to develop a grandiose part of their personality that sees anyone different from itself as an enemy.

Notwithstanding the very small number of groups considered and the absence of controls, the author identifies two types of dynamic in suicide terrorists: on one hand, there are "nationalist-separatists", who are profoundly loyal to their families and hate the regime that harms their loved ones and other members of their community; and, on the other, the "anarchic-ideologues" who are engaged in ongoing conflict with their families, which are, in effect, equated with the government they oppose.

Another pathologizing version of the suicide terrorist is offered by Robins and, again, Post (Robins & Post, 1997), who categorize these individuals as suffering from a paranoid syndrome. In these authors' view, grandiose and persecutory ideas combined with feelings of inadequacy fuel narcissistic rage, which, by virtue of a profound identification with the movement's leaders, causes them to embrace the "psychopolitics of hate".

One wonders whether such hypotheses, plausible as they may appear at first sight, are in fact specific to the terrorist movement, and, in particular, whether they are applicable to the dynamic of a suicide attacker. For example, many people engage in risky undertakings in an attempt to assert a deficient self. Again, it is not uncommon for the leader of a political movement to be a grandiose personality who reinforces the paranoid vision of his followers, but this is true of many political groups or movements that have never gone to the lengths of practising terrorism.

Among the pathologizers, the most extreme is Anderson (2004, quoted in Meneguz, 2005), who postulates that suicide terrorists suffer from neurological and structural brain defects, for instance in the frontal and temporal lobes and the amygdala. Anderson is a psychiatrist who has worked at the Guantánamo detention camp, which was set up in 2002 to hold prisoners of war suspected of terrorism.

An intermediate position is occupied by Silke (2003), who believes that suicide terrorists cannot readily be diagnosed with the symptoms of a mental disorder. In his view, these persons, while not presenting manifest individual psychopathology, are in fact insufficiently socialized: an individual who is poorly integrated in the community may become a terrorist if vengeful rage is triggered in him by, for example, an act of violence by the security forces against a friend, family member, or other acquaintance or associate.

Non-pathologizing versions

Contrary to the stereotype of the poor, maladapted terrorist or fanatical monster, the majority of suicide terrorists actually come from the cultivated or upper classes, have no sociopathic antecedents, and do not exhibit any kind of antisocial disorder. Having investigated the childhoods of 172 terrorist jihadis, Sageman (2004) concludes that only 8% of his sample (i.e., a third of the cases whose infantile histories could be reconstructed) displayed manifest behavioural disturbances in their early lives.

In general, young terrorists have middle-class backgrounds, and are brought up in religious families who have passed on their moral and spiritual values to them. Sageman considers that the fideistic espousal of martyrdom is attributable more to group ideology than to hatred of the enemy.

The only case involving possible mental pathology is that of Zacarias Moussaoui, indicted and tried in the United States as a member of the World Trade Center attack group. His brother's account of his life (Moussaoui & Bouquillat, 2002) clearly shows that, while living in London, Zacarias underwent a profound change of character: having previously been gentle and meek, he became gloomy and aggressive. Returning sporadically to his family, he became increasingly fanatical and polemical in his religious outlook and more and more quarrelsome, while closing off his mind in persecutory fashion. Eventually he disappeared, breaking off all links with his brother, to whom he had previously been very attached, and confined himself to occasional contacts, by telephone only, with his mother and sister. Zacarias's brother is convinced that he fell into the hands of the al-Qaeda organization, which was recruiting young people alienated from their families in London, and that he subsequently became a terrorist.

Granted that so-called normal people do not usually commit suicide, and that, if they do decide to do so, it is certainly not with a view to killing others, the rate of clinically ascertainable psychopathology in suicide terrorists is lower than the average for the population at large. Common sense confirms that suicide terrorists are not suffering from behavioural disorders. How could an individual with antisocial or criminal tendencies function in a terrorist type of organization, which calls for strict discipline and, in particular, involves a level of frustration and renunciation that even people with mature and well-structured personalities could not readily tolerate?

In his book *Inside Terrorism*, Hoffman (1998) maintains that individual terrorists are not insane fanatics, but thoughtful personalities who have made a rational choice after prolonged soul-searching.

All these psychodynamic considerations thus suggest that no single psychological pattern characterizes members of suicide terrorist movements (Horgan, 2003), and that in addressing the problem one must take due account of its historical, human, and environmental context.

This is borne out by the findings of Hassan (2001) in interviews with some 250 persons who had been in contact with suicide terrorists as family members or instructors in the Gaza Strip between 1996 and 1999. This author also managed to interview some terrorists who had been unable to complete their missions. He reports that none of the suicide terrorists in his sample, aged between eighteen and thirty-eight, conformed to the profile of the suicidal personality. All were well educated, and none was depressed or destitute. Many of the younger ones were from the middle class and, unless they had had to flee from the occupied territories, were in paid employment. Some came from Israeli territory. Two were the sons of wealthy families. They all belonged to normal nuclear families; some were regarded by their communities as model youngsters, religiously observant and well informed about the politics of the State of Israel and of the Arab world. Very many of them could recite long passages from the Koran by heart and were experts in Islamic law. All had intensely anti-Jewish views, and their knowledge of the Christian world was confined to the period of the Crusades.

The testimony of Nasra Hassan confirms that those intending to become suicide terrorists are apparently *normal* individuals. However, the fact that suicide has become a mass phenomenon can certainly not be regarded as normal.

First men and later women have made the decision to become human bombs, thus invalidating the belief (as expressed, for example, by psychoanalysts such as Chodorow (2003) that violence and the practice of terrorism are the prerogative of the male sex. Women too, although traditionally remote from politics and violence, subsequently joined in the perpetration of these massacres.

Cultural roots

How could this happen? What are the roots of the phenomenon, and what kind of political organization lies behind the suicide attackers? How did this culture come into being? Reuter (2002) contends that the practice of martyrdom in war began with the

Iranian suicide battalions. At the beginning of the 1980s, in the bloody Iran–Iraq conflict, tens of thousands of adolescents were sent to their deaths in the name of God and of Ayatollah Khomeini, cut down by the Iraqi machine-gunners while wearing little keys round their necks to assure them of access to Paradise. It was Khomeini himself who revived the sacrificial myths of Shi'ite Islam, inspired by the sacrifice of Imam Hussein at Karbala in the revolt against the caliphs. The notion of laying down one's life as a weapon of war was the nucleus of the future strategy of suicide: it was the Iranian Revolutionary Guards who exported this tactic to Lebanon, thus helping the Lebanese Shi'ites to form Hezbollah, the Party of God.

During the same period, some Muslim religious leaders broke with Islamic tradition and championed the practice of martyrdom in terrorist organizations. I shall mention just a few of these (cf. Khosrokhavar, 2003).

Even if the Koran forbids killing or the taking of one's own life, the theorists of Holy Death hold that there is an exception to this prohibition. They cite a well-known passage from the *Sura of Repentance* (Koran, 9: 112), according to which God has bought the lives and wealth of believers in exchange for Paradise. The faithful who slay and are slain in the name of God will have their reward. This passage from the *Sura of Repentance* is held to constitute the theoretical foundation of Islam's justification of martyrdom. However, as many religious exegetes have pointed out, the term *shahid* (martyr), which has become the key word in the justification of Holy Death, does not occur in this text. The Koranic precept seems to refer only to death at the hands of an enemy, and not to suicide with the aim of killing that enemy.

According to Motahhari, an important theorist of the justification of suicide terrorism, the martyr's merit is that of choosing death in order to allow others to continue to live a good life. By dying, he burns like a candle so as to give other people the light without which they would remain in darkness. Unlike those of others, his body is pure and does not require ritual ablution before interment.

For Ali Shari'ati, another eminent religious thinker, it is only in death that a Muslim can obtain the dignity that was denied him in life. The responsibility for the death of the young suicides is laid at the door of the imperialist, arrogant West, which has humiliated Muslim societies. It is the very material progress of the Western world that is likely to corrupt Muslim purity. By sacrificing himself, man, who is made from dirt but has a divine soul, plunges the base half of himself into the fire of faith and thereby becomes wholly divine.

In the last two decades, the invitation to die *in order to reconstruct the identity of the Muslim people* has become the watchword of the Islamic martyrs. As Khosrokhavar (2003) writes, Shari'ati theorized the impossibility of existence of the new generations who, owing to despotic or corrupt political structures (as in Palestine) and unjust global domination (by the United States of America), are justified in practising martyrdom as a new form of struggle. In martyrdom, the individual takes his life into his hands and sacrifices it for a transcendent cause; every good Muslim must take part in the Holy War by making the ultimate sacrifice.

Endorsement through religion

In strategic terms, the decision to use suicide terrorists first bore fruit in the attacks on the American and French troops stationed in Lebanon, which were thereby forced to withdraw. The five truck-bomb attacks in Lebanon in 1982 and 1983 claimed the lives of some 500 persons. In a single day, 23 October 1983, suicide attackers killed 248 American military personnel and 100 French paras (Fisk, 2005).

It was the Hezbollah movement in southern Lebanon that made *martyrdom* a deliberate instrument for securing the maximum effect with the minimum of sacrifice. The culture of martyrdom was subsequently endorsed even by religious leaders, notwithstanding all their doubts. Eventually, as stated above, the conviction prevailed that every good Muslim must take part in the Holy War and make the ultimate sacrifice. Only God knows when a given person must die, and all an individual can do is to choose the manner of his death.

Even if suicide is still frowned upon by religious law, exceptions are allowed where the purpose is sacred. In this way, the suicide attacker is first legitimized and then venerated as a martyr. Hence the seeming paradox that the groups favouring suicide attacks are those which also have a well structured social programme, in southern Lebanon they run schools, hospitals, and vocational training courses. Again, in the absence of these welfare facilities, it is quite likely that the strategy of voluntary martyrdom would not have gained acceptance and come to be seen as justified by the community.

Even if the Hezbollah group has progressively reduced the number of attacks almost to zero, it has nevertheless laid down the fundamental rules of procedure (including assistance and support for the martyr's family), and succeeded in publicizing them widely as if in a marketing campaign, thus encouraging risky imitation. The martyr with his explosive cargo has become a myth not only in the Arab world but also in Sri Lanka, Turkey, and Chechnya. Moreover, this myth has been disseminated and amplified by the contemporary media, even in the West.

As Reuter (2002) shows, the impact of a suicide attack stems not only from the act itself but also from the echo it arouses both in the attacker's society and in that of the victims, who must live with anxiety on a daily basis. As a result of the omnipresent Israeli roadblocks, the isolation of towns, and the precautionary assassination of movement leaders, which has also claimed innocent children among its victims, what can be described as a *culture of death* has developed in many strata of Palestinian society. The roadblocks, for example, have never constituted an effective security measure (they have apparently hardly ever intercepted a suicide attacker), but have certainly contributed to the ruin of the Palestinian economy; and when forced to wait for hours by a dusty roadside, wounded people in ambulances have sometimes succumbed to their injuries.

At times of crisis, the action of human bombs has reinforced the idea of a community prepared for universal sacrifice in response to enemy onslaught, and fuelled the myth of the hero in that community.

Ritualization of sacrifice

The terrorist groups who use, or have used, suicide attackers can be classified in two main groups.

The first comprises sectarian organizations, which do not permit their members to have a life outside the group. The individual is not autonomous; it is the group leaders who decide when he must die for the cause. This was the organizational structure of the Kurdish PKK before Abdullah Öcalan decreed its end, and, with a few differences, it was also that of the Tamil Tigers (LTTE), who carried out at least 170 suicide attacks from 1987 on.

In these sectarian organizations, the young suicide-attackers-to-be are indoctrinated in special training camps, isolated from the rest of the community. From then on, it is impossible for them to quit and to disobey the order to complete the suicide mission. The Kurdish women who have carried out attacks on behalf of the PKK, once chosen, could not refuse and had to complete their missions, as they would otherwise have been rejected by their communities as widows. These women had no possibility of standing aloof from the guerrilla movement, the only haven and source of protection in isolated, dangerous areas of virtual desert.

The situation of communities that implicitly embrace the policy of suicide attacks is very different. These communities include the former Lebanese groups and those acting within certain Palestinian organizations (for instance, those controlled by Hamas). Such an attack was seen as a sacrificial death approved and supported by the entire community; it was held up as an example and followed by other youngsters of the same age.

Hamas and Jihad recruited volunteers for martyrdom attacks only among young people, but did not accept minors under the age of eighteen, sole family breadwinners, or married individuals. Candidates were first scrutinized to confirm their religious zeal and self-discipline; then, in the fortnight before the mission, they were entrusted to two assistants who were constantly in attendance and required to take note of the slightest expression of uncertainty. In the event of any doubts, a more expert trainer was called in to help the candidate to overcome the difficulty.

It is perhaps bewildering to see the pictures of parents receiving congratulations for their sons' martyrdom. It is hard to say whether they really do accept the choice of the ultimate sacrifice, or whether they simply feel that it is their duty to show pride in their offspring, in order not to betray their memory and not to make their sacrifice appear futile.

The conviction of being able to live on in Paradise does not seem to play a decisive part in suicide attacks. (According to Argo (2006), the statistics show that almost half of suicide attacks before 2003 were carried out by political rather than religious terrorist organizations.) Nor has the prospect of the pleasure awaiting in the form of virgins in the Muslim Paradise always proved particularly attractive. For instance, Mohammed Atta was misogynistic to the point of leaving instructions that no woman was to be allowed to visit his grave. He is therefore unlikely to have been tempted by the idea of being cheered in Paradise by the presence of seventy-two virgins. What in fact attracted him was the purifying power of death: he had copied the relevant passages from the Koran into his diary. A more important motivation, also declared by the same death volunteer, is the expectation of remaining in the community's memory and of being seen as a hero. As Meneguz (2005) rightly notes, whether an act is seen as *terrorism* or as *heroism* is a matter of one's emotional standpoint. In 1706, Pietro Micca, a miner enlisted in the Savoyard army, blew himself up on a mine, killing the French troops who were about to enter Turin. In Italian history books he is a hero, but from another point of view he could be deemed a suicide terrorist.

A Hamas militant interviewed by Reuter (2002) described the last hours of a suicide-to-be. The last night is devoted to prayer; if he has debts, he repays them; before embarking on the action, he repeats the pre-prayer ritual ablution, shaves, dresses in clean clothes, and, if possible, prays one last time in the mosque, where he begs forgiveness for his sins. He slips a small Koran into his pocket and puts on his explosive belt. No one in his family is aware of his intention, which also remains unknown to his friends and even to the other members of the organization. Only those belonging to the small cell entrusted with the preparation of the attack know about it.

As soon as the attacker has completed his mission, the organization distributes video cassettes containing his last will and testament, which are sold and commented on in mosques or at other meeting places.

In those organizations where decisions are taken by the leadership, the "chosen" suicide is also accorded privileged treatment before the sacrificial act. For instance, young Tamil Tiger suicides-to-be (the majority of whom were in fact women) had the honour of taking their last meal with the organization's supreme leader. The Hindu religion does not promise an afterlife, and therefore no celestial reward was expected, unlike the situation with their Islamic brethren. In this case too, however, after their sacrifice the martyrs were remembered with full honours and their families were proud of them.

A conspicuous difference between the Tamil Tigers and Islamic guerrillas was that the proportion of female suicide terrorists in the former group, at some sixty per cent, was higher than that of their male counterparts.

Among Öcalan's Kurdish independence fighters too, the percentage of women engaging in suicide missions was greater than that of men. The Marxist-Leninist PKK, fighting the Turkish Government for the independence of Kurdistan, used suicide terrorism to weaken the enemy, to sap enemy morale, and as propaganda for its cause among the international community. Its suicide attackers were selected by the organization.

The missions ended by the decision of the organization's political leader, Abdullah Öcalan, after his capture by the Turkish Government. Like the Tamil Tigers, the Kurds did not have a conception of Paradise for the martyr, but came to venerate the leader who sent them on their mission.

A political choice

Warfare involving human bombs began in specific circumstances and with a specific aim. As stated earlier, the first suicide terrorist attacks took place in Lebanon in the early 1980s with the aim of liberation from occupying troops. It is important to note that the conditions under which Lebanese citizens were then living were very different from those of the populations of Palestine or Chechnya. In Lebanon, the need was for liberation from foreign troops who stood in the way of political aims, which they opposed. In view of the risk run by the occupying nations of exposing their troops to fresh devastating attacks, this form of warfare proved successful. Hence the first suicide missions formed part of a limited political objective, and they were acts decided on from above by the

Muslim leadership of Hezbollah. Whereas suicide attacks were, as we have seen, not originally a mass phenomenon, over time this tactic came to involve the entire community. It became a shared choice, approved and seen as just by many, irrespective of sex, age, or religious ideals.

How then did suicide terrorism come to be so consolidated as to become a widespread practice? Considering Palestine alone, it took a long period of war and bloody conflict between Palestinians and Israelis to convince the former that they could achieve more by death than by life. What mattered for the community was to emerge from its state of resignation.

Revenge for the loss of relatives and friends at the hands of the enemy accounts for the choice of some of these suicides. This may perhaps have been the motivation of the Chechen women who sacrificed themselves after their husbands had died under the Russian army's repression. After all, in certain Muslim groups, widows are often cast out of the community. This may explain the action of Zarina Alikhanova, the Chechen suicide terrorist who died in the Znamenskoye attack of 12 May 2003, one of the bloodiest on record, which cost the lives of sixty people (Source: www.cesnur.org/2004/waco_introvigne.htm, accessed May 2010). Zarina had been a model student and a passionate ballet dancer. After her husband, a leading Chechen guerrilla, was killed by the Russians, she joined the terrorist organization and was willing to lay down her own life in order to avenge his death.

The Japanese kamikaze

In spite of the differences in culture and historical context, one is surprised at certain resemblances between the subjective behaviour of the Japanese kamikaze and that of present-day suicide terrorists.[3] Although the Japanese kamikaze were military personnel and their targets were not civilian populations—that would have been seen as dishonourable—their ceremonies and pre-death state of mind resembled those of the Muslim martyrs. According to Ivan Morris (1975), the members of the kamikaze units were far from being the ferocious, fanatical nationalists portrayed by the Western press. From all the testimonies and materials available to the historian (letters, photographs, and diaries), the most common type of individual was a calm, serious young man, of above-average culture and sensitivity. The kamikaze-to-be (whether pilots or naval personnel) were not subjected to any pressure to join the suicide squadrons and did not receive any special indoctrination, although the possibility cannot be ruled out that some younger elements may have succumbed to psychological pressure from their companions. When the air force or naval corps adopted the kamikaze method, the members of the existing units were free to decide for themselves whether to take part in suicide missions. On the mental turmoil preceding the decision to sacrifice one's life, Morris reports the testimony of Captain Nakajima, who, after a period of melancholia, found his serenity restored once he had resolved to die: life coincided with death, and mortality with immortality.

What drove thousands of young Japanese to lay down their lives? Their letters, diaries, and poems indicate that hatred of the enemy and the wish to avenge their dead companions were not the most significant factors. What sent them to their deaths was the debt of gratitude they felt they owed the country in which they had grown up and which was now in mortal danger; they were proud of the history and mythology of Japan, and in particular grateful to the figure of the Emperor, who embodied the virtue and unity of the fatherland. The same sense of gratitude was also often displayed towards their families at the last farewell.

Even though the tactics of suicide were presented as the only possible way of saving Japan from catastrophe, not very many kamikaze seem to have really believed this. Yet, far from undermining their morale, the manifest ineffectiveness of certain attacks merely galvanized them to even greater efforts. They identified with the country's fate to such an extent as to equate their own death with its imminent demise. They thought that, if Japan was doomed to be defeated, their sacrifice would foreshadow its spiritual rebirth.

In joining the suicide units, they were already imbued with the idealization of death borrowed from the samurai ethic, which saw suicide not as a form of flight, but as a proud and worthy act and the only honourable way out of a hopeless situation.

In reality, Japanese pilots in those last, desperate days of the war were already confronting death at every instant, and may have been actively seeking it out partly in order to strip it of its anxiety-inducing power. Death would not then come from outside or by chance, but would supervene as an act of will.

CHAPTER FOUR

Martyrdom and the sadomasochistic link

"We will succeed whether we live or die. Death will defi-
nitely come one day. . . . It does not matter whether we die
today or tomorrow. The goal is martyrdom"

(Mullah Muhammad Omar, Taliban leader in
Afghanistan, quoted in *New York Times*, 18 October 2001)

Christian martyrdom

In the Arab world, the term "martyr" was originally reserved for
non-combatants or civilians who fell victim to the enemy (Argo,
2006). In this sense, the Muslim connotation of a martyr can be
seen as resembling its Christian counterpart, because the element of
aggression is lacking in both cases. The Muslim community considered a martyr to be anyone who innocently sacrificed himself for
the benefit of those who had fallen before him or might fall in the
future. However, to what extent is the sacrifice of a suicide terrorist
really similar to that of a Christian martyr?

In the Christian tradition, martyrdom is a profession of faith
that may extend even unto death. The word "martyr" (from the

Greek for a witness) denotes someone who bears witness to his faith even if it entails the loss of his life. Christians persecuted by the Roman emperors could save themselves from death by abjuring their faith.

Although the genre of the *passio* in vogue in the Middle Ages suggested that martyrs sacrificed themselves spontaneously, even when they could have avoided doing so, this does not seem to reflect the reality of the situation. At times of persecution, Christians had only two options: either to abjure their faith and pay tribute to the emperor, or to die.

There are many Christian anecdotes about martyrs who were not prepared to abjure their faith and who died bearing witness to it. For instance, at the time when the emperor Licinius was persecuting the Christians in Armenia, forty legionaries declared their allegiance to Christianity. Their punishment was to be forced to strip naked and to stand in a frozen pond; however, if they were prepared to abjure their faith, they could find shelter in a nearby hut. While some calmly awaited death on the ice, many continued to pray. One member of the group, unable to endure the suffering any longer, headed for the hut. The soldier standing watch, having admitted him, then decided to take his place on the frozen lake. Eventually the cold claimed the lives of all forty of the soldiers who were thereby intent on bearing witness to their faith in Christianity.

In other words, Christian martyrdom was characterized by the refusal to submit to Caesar's commands; death decreed by authority is the consequence of the Christian's insubordination. However, even if death is not desired, a possible change of meaning is implicit in the very idea of martyrdom. Death undergone out of loyalty to one's creed can readily blend into a wish to lay down one's life in order to attain the paradise of God's elect.

Whereas the Christian martyr accepted his end with resignation and saw it as a liberation, the situation of someone who actively seeks death is quite different. This was the case with the aspiration to martyrdom that became widespread in certain Catholic religious communities suffering an identity crisis during the Counter-Reformation. We in the West should not be too surprised—while not underestimating its dangers—at the propaganda function of the madrasas or of certain Islamic religious communities inflamed by the fiery preaching of some imams.

In the sixteenth century, the Catholic world was in the throes of a severe religious and political crisis. National communities were threatened from within by hate and religious fanaticism on the Catholic and Protestant sides alike; the very survival of the Catholic Church and the institution of the pontificate seemed to be at risk. To preserve the continuity of Catholicism's politico-religious institutions, some important organizations were established, the most famous and effective of which was the Society of Jesus, founded by Ignatius of Loyola. The Society was promptly recognized by the Pope and given the resources to consolidate itself and to take immediate action when necessary.

The Colleges, in which large numbers of young people were instructed and educated to combat the Protestant heresy, were an executive arm of the Society. Some of them secretly infiltrated the Protestant nations, such as England, with the aim of conversion. When discovered, they were cruelly tortured and finally killed. The gruesome fate of the unfortunate missionaries did not diminish the zeal of the Society's followers.[4]

The following description of the recruits' state of mind was given by a visitor to the English College of the Society of Jesus in Rome:

> So eager are they to shed their blood for Christ that this forms the constant topic of their conversation. Many would shorten the time of their studies to be free to rush into the fray . . . when the news is brought from England of some fresh outbreak of heretical rage and cruelty, it enkindles the desire to undergo in their turn the like afflictions and tortures. [Wright, 2004, p. 30]

As is apparently demonstrated by the historical experience of the ideological struggle between the various religious factions at the time of the Counter-Reformation, the perception of a threat to one's identity and identification of the other as the enemy can lead to the apotheosis of sacrifice. However, a threat to identity, by itself, does not suffice to explain the creation of a sacrificial state of mind. It is, in my view, necessary to emphasize the process of idealization that precedes it. The love object becomes so ideal that its survival— or rather, its affirmation—calls for total submission.

This process of idealization is similar to that of the Japanese kamikaze martyrs. The human is thus sacrificed to the ideal, and self-immolation for the sake of the idealized object is accompanied by sensory pleasure and excitation.

Destruction of the enemy through an individual's death already features in religious myth. For instance, Samson brings down the temple, taking as many of the enemy as possible with him to the grave. The attacker knows that he will not eliminate the enemy once and for all, but will inflict a wound or laceration on the enemy's body, thus triggering an unremitting sequence of acts of retaliation and revenge. His aim is to increase the level of hatred in a potentially infinite sadomasochistic circuit. There are many possible forms of identification with the aggressor, which may be fuelled by the profanation of religion or of the attacker's country, or by the indelible memory of the suffering of his co-religionists in Guantánamo or Abu Ghraib.

Sadomasochistic withdrawal

The following brief digression into the field of clinical psychoanalysis indicates the kind of psychopathological model that might be relevant to the disturbing evolution of a suicide terrorist.

Infantile traumas may have different adult outcomes depending on the subject's propensity for violent reaction. In some cases, trauma may inhibit the patient's emotional development, so that he withdraws from affective relationships and seemingly lives without emotions. Such patients lack emotional awareness of the facts of the past; however, the memory of the trauma is preserved in the unconscious and may then appear in dreams or the transference even though the patient is not clearly conscious of it.

Some patients, on the other hand, betray the traumas they have suffered from the very beginning of their therapy. They offer a detailed description of their parents' character and deficiencies and of the injustices to which they have been subjected. Sometimes they seem to take careful note of all their wrongs, whether inevitable or accidental, in order to work themselves up to a pitch of resentment and violence. The analyst's emotional involvement is no comfort, but in fact appears to magnify their complaints. By thus expressing the suffering of the past, the patient adds fuel to his position as a victim and his aggression grows apace.

The leitmotif in the analysis of Carmen, a young woman of South American origin, consists of accusations directed against her parents, and in particular her mother, whose emotional distance triggers violent rages in the daughter. Carmen, however, is tied to her mother, by a twofold bond, in a relationship of both psychological subjection and total dependence. In her everyday life too, the patient encounters people who prove to be tyrannical and violent; an attempted relationship eventually became characterized by perversion, involving constant physical and mental violence to which she seems to have submitted passively.

Yet, it is mainly her relationship with her mother, with whom she still lives, that constitutes the principal source of the sadomasochistic storms. Carmen recently had to travel to another town by train and asked her mother for money for a taxi as she would be coming home late. When her mother refused, the patient did not object, but apparently accepted her decision. However, as soon as she left the train she felt invaded by violence:

> "When I got off the train, I didn't have enough money for a taxi and I couldn't remember where to get the bus. I went down into the station forecourt and it was dark. I saw a group of drunken Africans who were throwing beer bottles at each other. The thing is, I was absolutely not afraid of the gang . . . I could have avoided them and gone a different way, but instead I went right into their midst . . . How shall I put it . . . it had already happened to me once, so it could easily have happened again. That's also what I do when I cut myself . . . it's like being in a concentration camp, when you become an emotionless object . . ."

In this situation, the patient is more interested in showing how bad the world is (the world being represented by men and her mother) than in defending her physical integrity; she finds it more pleasurable to provoke aggression than to protect herself. Offering herself up as a potential rape victim is an expression of her persistent masochistic fury and of her role as a victim of aggression.

Anna is a patient who is seriously ill. She has had episodes of anorexia since early childhood. The first trauma was a pyloric dysfunction that occurred in the early months of her life, resulting in feeding difficulties due to vomiting, which her family noticed only at a late stage (they thought the little girl was just being naughty). During her adolescence, the patient was hospitalized several times on account of serious anorexic episodes, and therapeutic community placements were also tried on several occasions so as to remove her from a family environment characterized by mutual rage and ambivalence, involving her mother in particular.

Her relationships with those near and dear to her have always been precarious, if not catastrophic, with suicide threats and attempts that also resulted in hospitalization. The wealth of symptoms she displays include panic attacks and periods of anorexia punctuated by bulimic orgies. Her latest admission to hospital is quite recent, following a suicide attempt with prescribed drugs.

On returning to analysis, she tells me that her act of self-harm was due to a profound failure of understanding with her husband and the fact that, as usual, the only way she could manage conflict is by self-destructive behaviour. The interval following this storm lasts only a few days, her sessions immediately being filled with threats and declarations of possible violence: for example, she proposes plunging from the window or taking another overdose. Once again she gets up at the crack of dawn so as to spend an hour running wildly, and arrives for her sessions out of breath on her bicycle when she could perfectly well have used public transport. In this way she has lost even the little additional weight that had made her gaunt appearance less alarming. She cannot sleep, feels depressed, has fantasies of suicide, and says she wants to go into hospital.

I tell her that her self-destructiveness has broken out once more. Apparently surprised, she admits that she got angry with her husband again when she felt him to be emotionally aloof from her, and that she hates her mother, who makes a show of indifference. She claims to be fascinated by the idea of going into hospital—a place of refuge, a womb to which she can return in bliss.

What is happening in Anna's mind? Lacking a space of her own, in order to survive she must remain indissolubly bound to her objects (her mother, her husband, and her analyst). The old sado-masochistic link, which was responsible for her severe anorexic symptoms in adolescence, is still active and resurfaces with every frustration, although she is not aware of it. The attack on the object is inflicted not with vital rage but with self-destructiveness: like a suicide terrorist, Anna hurls her body at the hated object in order to strike a blow at it and to involve it in her self-destructiveness. For this patient, the self-annihilating urge is the destructive response to the early, unbearable trauma and rage; anorexia is a mental strategy directed towards self-destruction that includes a violent attack on the bodily self and on the frustrating object, in a dynamic of endless repetition.

I have described these two patients' sadomasochistic links with a view to establishing a possible analogy with the destructiveness of young terrorists. According to this hypothesis, hatred of the enemy assumes a perverse configuration in which the sadistic pleasure of killing ultimately coincides with that of masochistic self-annihilation.

Although this model may help us to understand the evolution of a suicide attacker, it is by no means exhaustive. The sado-masochistic motivation of the two patients described above more closely resembles that of an attacker imbued with destructive hate and prepared to sacrifice his life if only he can thereby exterminate the enemy. This was the situation of Baruch Goldstein, the doctor and settler mentioned earlier, who was responsible for the carnage at the Cave of the Patriarchs in 1994 and who deliberately set out to kill as many Palestinians as possible before being killed himself. Baruch's state of mind may perhaps be likened to that of a concentration camp inmate who has had enough of the humiliation and torment inflicted by his torturers and decides to hurl himself at his persecutors, killing as many of them as possible and dying himself in the process. His can be seen as a case of murder–suicide, even if, strictly speaking, Baruch did not take his own life, but was eventually killed by someone else.

CHAPTER FIVE

Murder–suicide

"Thou . . . who hast dared to plunge the sword in thine own
children, . . . and hast destroyed me childless"

(Euripides, *Medea*, 2008)

Murder–suicide in the family

Murder–suicide is a not infrequent phenomenon that has been the subject of many criminological studies. It occurs when the murderer commits suicide after killing his victim, and presupposes a link between the two protagonists; for this reason, it is most frequent in couples or families. There are, however, cases in which the murderer takes the lives of people outside the family context—for example, workmates or school-mates—or turns his aggression on unwitting passers-by.

A masterly description of murder–suicide is given in Carrère's book *The Adversary* (2000) and the film based on it. The novel is inspired by the true story of Jean-Claude Romand, who has succeeded in lying to his parents and friends for eighteen years, making them believe that he is a brilliant physician. He marries and continues the deception with his wife. Pretending to work for the World Health Organization in Geneva, Jean-Claude spends his days driving around aimlessly or visiting motels, to pass the time before rejoining his wife and children in the evenings. Eventually the game is up and he is about to be unmasked, so he takes the only action possible for his sick ego—eliminating everyone who might suffer or condemn him for being an impostor. Jean-Claude resolves to kill his wife and children and then to commit suicide, thus transforming the prolonged farce into tragedy.

Statistics show that children are the most frequent victims of murder–suicide. Like Medea, some parents decide to commit suicide after taking their children's lives. A high proportion of those who commit this crime are women, whose aim in killing their children is usually to hurt their partners.

Besides this type of murder–suicide, which is carried out under the banner of hate, there is another, called mercy killing. It happens when someone kills the person he loves, rightly or wrongly seen as suffering with no hope of recovery, and then takes his own life. Such cases often occur in old age, when people feel that they have no future.

Some suicides have taken place after massacres of groups of anonymous individuals who had no personal connection with the murderer. When the perpetrator does not spontaneously take his own life, he is ultimately killed himself.

Mass slaughter

An instance of mass slaughter that ended with the death of the protagonists took place at the Columbine High School in Colorado. On 20 April 1999, two students, Eric Harris, aged eighteen, and Dylan Klebold, aged seventeen, entered the school at West Denver, Colorado, armed with carbines and bombs, and, having killed twelve students and a teacher, committed suicide. Their story has been told in two films, *Bowling for Columbine*, by Michael Moore (2002), and *Elephant*, by Gus Van Sant (2003).

As with suicide attackers, for these two young people death was the price to pay for killing. According to notes subsequently posted online by the Denver police, they had prepared the massacre well in advance, even divulging their intention at school. Both were very isolated and friendless. From a certain point on, their diaries include slogans and symbols of Nazi propaganda, expressions of admiration for the serial killer Charles Manson, and drawings of mutilated or wounded people. Harris writes that he wanted to kill all his schoolmates save those who were isolated like himself: "I have a goal to destroy as much as possible so I must not be side-tracked by my feelings of sympathy, mercy, or any of that . . . I'm full of hate and I love it" (source: http://acolumbinesite.com/eric/writing/journal.html, accessed May 2010). Nowhere in the diary, on the other hand, is there any mention of suicide; instead, it seems that the pair had planned to escape from the school to a foreign country. A possible alternative was to hijack a plane and crash it down on the city of New York. However, following the massacre, they committed suicide to avoid capture.

The two young Americans' victims were a group of hated people. The difference between the two students and suicide terrorists is that the former were excited by killing, loved blood, and wanted to shed it. What held sway over their minds and steered them towards the carnage was the wish to kill. For this reason, the two American youngsters, who sought revenge for the wrongs they felt had been inflicted on them, were totally identified with the destructive figures of Nazis or serial killers. A suicide attacker, on the other hand, does not hate. He places his life in the service of the community with which he is wholly identified; he acts in the name of the group and not out of personal hatred. Even where his history includes a traumatic memory, such as the deaths of family members, he is not wreaking private vengeance like the protagonists of the Columbine High School massacre.

The young Pakistanis responsible for the attacks on the London Underground in 2005 were not traumatized; born in England, they were seemingly well integrated in society. Unlike co-religionists living in war-torn territories, these young people had no obvious reason to hate the society in which they lived.[5] Their act cannot have been motivated by the aim of avenging the suffering caused by the occupation.

As Usuelli (2006) writes, a second-generation terrorist is not driven by hate; he is apparently integrated into the Western world, but, by virtue of an ethnic conflict or affective trauma, is plunged into an identity crisis whereby he attributes his woes to having to live in the contemporary atheistic and materialistic world. A possible way out of this existential crisis seems to be the espousal of a religious creed, in which doubt and anxiety are banished by the black-and-white distinction between the good and the not-good. The author contrasts indoctrination, involving a large number of the faithful, with paramilitary training, which is probably targeted at selected individuals considered more likely to undertake violent action.

The majority of second-generation immigrants in the West integrate and accept the lifestyle of the society around them. Just a small number develop an implacable antagonism to the West, and it is from these groups that the individuals destined to be recruited by terrorist networks originate. They feel oppressed by the political and cultural hegemony of a colonizing superpower over the Holy Land of Islam (the basing of US troops in Saudi Arabia after the Gulf War) or supporting countries in conflict with the Muslims (e.g. Israel and the Palestinians). These individuals see themselves as spokespersons for an unhappy Muslim consciousness that accuses the West of insensitivity and hostility.

One of the London suicide terrorists, Mohammed Sidique Khan, recorded the following words in a video: "Your democratically elected governments continuously perpetrate atrocities against my people all over the world. . . . Until we feel security, you will be our targets" (*Daily Telegraph*, London, 2 September 2005).

The suicidal vocations of second-generation terrorists in fact have a much more complex pattern of psychological development. These individuals are probably seduced by the idea of sacrifice because they have long been fascinated by extreme solutions. Despite their seeming integration, they have cultivated and shared a "parallel world" remote from reality and banefully close to the apocalyptic visions of certain Muslim leaders (Stapley, 2006).[6]

CHAPTER SIX

The network and filicide

"Suicide–mass murder is more than terrorism: it is horror-ism. It is a maximum malevolence"
(Martin Amis, quoted in *Observer*, London, 10 September 2006)

The gerontocracy

Some forty years ago, Arnaldo Rascovsky, one of the pioneers of the Latin American psychoanalytic movement, wrote a stimulating book entitled *Filicide* (1973). In his analysis of the phenomenon of war, the author maintains that one of its aims is to cause the new generations to fight among themselves. In his view, war is the cyclic expression of an initiation rite that demands the sacrifice of the upcoming generation. The decision to go to war is never taken by the generations that take part in it, but instead by the senile minds that hold power. Death in war is imbued with a powerful moral connotation, accompanied by preservation of the innocence of the gerontocracy responsible for it. The young people concerned are honoured if they identify with their fathers' commands and kill others of their own age, but if they attempt to desert, they are deemed to be criminals. The elders who send their off-spring to their deaths hide behind a symbolic abstraction called the fatherland, which demands the voluntary sacrifice of the young people's lives. The fathers conceal their own destructiveness and compel their sons to engage in self-idealization with the aim of denying the true nature of their filicide.

In the present age of suicide terrorism, filicide has become so manifest that it can dispense with its traditional mask. The fathers openly call upon their sons to sacrifice themselves and the sons accept their will. The young people sent to the slaughter do not oppose those who dictate their fate (the older generation).[7] A terrorist attacker introjects the destructive will of the gerontocracy—that is, of the minds at the summit of a strongly ideologized power structure. Idealization of the cause blots out the perception of the massacre, emphasizes the beauty of martyrdom, and turns suicide bombing into a *fact of everyday life*.

The phenomenon of suicide terrorism is not specific to the Islamic world. At the time of the evacuation of Israeli soldiers and settlers from Gaza, a group of young Israeli citizens aged between twenty-five and thirty-five pronounced themselves willing to blow themselves up in order to kill ministers in their own government of whose policies they disapproved. Their heroes were Baruch Goldstein, mentioned earlier, and Yigal Amir, who assassinated Prime Minister Rabin in November 1995. In this case, suicide terrorism seems to have found converts even among those ideologically opposed to the Islamic world.

Why did the will to engage in terrorism, latent in the young Israeli settlers, not become a political mass movement in their country as it did in Islamic society? Contemporary terrorism could not exist without a network of minds, such as *al-Qaeda*, as its foundation (*al-Qaeda* means "the base"). Suicide candidates meet, are selected, and enabled to act by this network. Israel does not have a network capable of organizing suicide terrorism, and in the absence of this relationship between would-be attackers and a network, there is also no idealization of sacrifice. In general, in the case of wars fought without ideals, young people are ultimately no longer prepared to acquiesce in the aims of the gerontocracy.

Well over four thousand American soldiers have been killed and more than twenty thousand wounded in Iraq, leading to an ever-wider gulf between fathers and sons. This is borne out by a collective letter to Congress from over a hundred American soldiers calling for an undertaking to withdraw the troops from Iraq. Whereas the American nation is beginning to see the sacrifice of human lives as manifestly futile filicide, a similar awareness is unlikely to arise on the opposing side. For suicide martyrs, death is a royal road leading straight from martyrdom to glory and to God.

To understand why suicide terrorism arose in some regions of the world and not in others, it must be remembered that certain peoples remote from our Western tradition have developed a different conception of death. In our culture, death is denied and exorcized as a source of anxiety about which we would rather remain ignorant; left unmourned and unworked-through emotionally, it forms part of the technological schematism of our age.

This is not the case in other cultures. Death is present during the course of existence and is not seen as a terrifying caesura of life; the afterlife itself is deemed to be a continuation of earthly life, and sometimes as the end of pain and suffering, rather than as the agonizing loss of affective life and personal identity.

The search for Paradise

Paradise Now, shown at the Berlin film festival in 2005 where it received awards and accolades, is a film by Hany Abu-Assad, a Palestinian director based in the Netherlands. Eschewing all rhetoric and dryly forceful in style, it tells the story of two young Palestinians who decide to die in a terrorist attack. Abu-Assad's film, which displays his profound knowledge of his land and people, is based on statements by champions of kamikaze-type attacks who escaped death, either because their explosives failed to detonate or because at the last minute they lacked the courage to blow themselves up.

The film portrays the final forty-eight hours in the lives of two Palestinian suicide terrorists. Said and Khaled are close friends living in Nablus, who suffer every day from being out of work, from the degradation of the environment and society, and from continuous humiliation by the Israeli army. Hatred of the occupation troops and the wish to take revenge are growing all around them. The two of them jointly decide to become suicide attackers. The day comes when the leader of the terrorist cell tells them that they have been chosen for a mission: they should be proud of the recognition shown to them. They spend their last few hours with their families, concealing their intention, dining with them, and sleeping at home in their own beds. Next day, at the house where the terrorist cell is accommodated, they receive instructions for their mission.

Dressed, shaven, and with their hair cut so that they look like Jewish settlers, they are washed and saluted by their companions, as appropriate for someone embarking on a journey of no return. They record their political testament on video and leave more personal communications for their families. Having eaten their last meal with their companions, they receive the blessing of the organization's leader.

While on their way to the attack site, they endeavour to support and strengthen each other in their resolve: they tell themselves that, although they will die, continuing to live in their situation is tantamount to being already dead; there is no way of stopping the Israeli oppressors except by striking a lasting blow at them. They are doing the right thing, they are heroes, and they will meet again on high, in heaven; as soon as they are dead, two angels will come down to earth and carry them off to Paradise.

With the aid of an accomplice, they enter Israeli territory, but are immediately intercepted; they therefore take flight and lose each other. Khaled returns to base. Said hides and decides to penetrate the barrier again in order to carry out the attack alone; however, while preparing to blow up a bus, he stops in his tracks on seeing the face of a child, and changes his mind.

Meanwhile, the terrorist cell is extremely worried. Said has disappeared and not a word has been heard from him; perhaps he has betrayed them, either willingly or under coercion. Khaled is given permission to search for his friend, whose loyalty he does not doubt.

The terse and dramatic dialogue between Khaled and Suha, a young woman from outside the occupied territories who is fond of Said, is the high point of the story. Having sensed the two young men's sacrificial intentions, she angrily condemns their crazy project. The suicide attack, she says, is merely a desperate act that can only worsen the desolation, make the Israeli army even crueller, and increase the level of persecution. What a tragic illusion it is to believe that causing such carnage is the road to Paradise! Paradise exists only in the minds of the attackers!

Khaled replies that unending injustice cannot be tolerated, and that it is better to have Paradise in one's mind and to die than to go on living in moral wretchedness and oppression. At least in death, oppressors and oppressed will be equal!

This dramatic exchange of ideas slowly begins to exercise Khaled's mind, increasingly worried as he is about Said's fate. He and Suha eventually find Said in the cemetery, lying prostrate on the grave of his father, who has been executed by the Palestinian resistance movement on charges of collaboration with the Israelis. Said intended to carry out the attack partly to redeem the figure of his father and to punish those who had driven him to betray his people; stretched out on the grave, he feels rage against the occupiers rising inside him and is determined to avenge his father's death.

Khaled, on the other hand, has begun to question his own choice after the confrontation with Suha, and tries to persuade his friend too not to go on. However, by means of a trick, Said slips away from his friend and his entreaties, and proceeds to the attack location on his own. Full of hate, he sets off to meet his death, and this time does not miss his target.

Why does Said die, while Khaled eschews the terrorist solution? What is the difference between the two friends?

Khaled's decision is motivated by the need to avenge the humiliation inflicted on his people and to take his leave of an increasingly meaningless life. He questions his political choices when his relationship with the terrorist organization, which suspects Said of betrayal, begins to crumble. Suha's position, dismissing the choice of suicide as counterproductive and likely to perpetuate the people's suffering indefinitely, helps him to think of an alternative approach to their struggle.

Said, for his part, is driven by pain and rage with deeper emotional roots. He must compensate for the betrayal by his father, who was unable to fight for his community's ideals and sold out to the enemy. Although Said loves and idealizes his father, he cannot comprehend his painful fate. Dealing in paranoid fashion with his disappointment at the realization of his father's weakness, he places all the blame on the shoulders of the Israeli enemy, seen as guilty of forcing his father to betray his people. His father has, in fact, betrayed not only the community but also his own son, and that is what Said cannot accept. The group of unwitting Israeli citizens slain in the attack become the scapegoats of this drama with no possible resolution.

CHAPTER SEVEN

The female suicide bomber

ISMENE: Yea, O king, such reason as nature may have given
abides not with the unfortunate, but goes astray

(Sophocles, *Antigone* (trans. R. C. Jebb)

Conferment of sainthood

Hiba's family was baffled when she insisted on covering herself from head to toe in an all-enveloping robe that left only her eyes exposed (Ghazali, 2003). The nineteen-year-old was studying English literature at Al Quds Open University in Tubas, in the West Bank. She never spoke to her male fellow-students and she avoided the cafeteria where the young people socialized. Not even her cousin, a young man studying at the same university, had ever seen her face uncovered or been able to talk to her. When they met, they never even shook hands. He saw her face for the first time in a poster released by Islamic Jihad after her death.

Hiba blew herself up in a shopping mall at Afula, in northern Israel, killing three Israelis and seriously wounding forty-eght. One of the victims was the female security guard who had tried to stop her entering the building.

On the previous day, Hiba had risen early, said her prayers, and made breakfast for her family. Her mother remembers that she went into the garden to water the plants, with a smile on her face as she smelt the roses. Asked why she was smiling, the daughter had replied: "I feel that I am a new person. You will be very proud of me." Before leaving town, she had visited her two sisters, returned a notebook to a classmate, and said goodbye to her grandfather.

When she detonated her explosive belt, Hiba had abandoned her Islamic clothes in favour of a pair of jeans, the better to disguise herself. Her family claimed to know nothing of her plans and said they were proud of her, the fifth heroine of the intifada. Only her grandmother disagreed, regretting her death and blaming those who recruited her, saying "She was too young." The family then lost their house, which was dynamited by the Israeli army.

Before killing herself, Hiba was devoutly religious; she seemed obsessed by the notion of sin, and would immediately turn off the radio if a love song was playing. She had been a model student, would pray for hours on end, and read the Koran. While repeating its verses she said she felt unique. Her oldest sister had continued to believe that she wanted to be a special person, both in her studies and in her religious aspirations. But she had not realized that Hiba wanted to be unique *in death*.

A psychiatrist, Ahmed Abu Tawahina, explained that the roadblocks and incursions by the Israeli army, the martyrs' funerals, the eulogies recited by militants, the graffiti, and the cult of suicide terrorism formed part of the political environment that constantly nourished the suicidal vocation of young Palestinians. In his view, then, the traumatic and inhuman conditions in which many of those youngsters were compelled to live were one of the reasons—perhaps the most important reason—for their choosing to end their lives in this way. However, this explanation places insufficient emphasis on the subjective factors that appear to have underlain Hiba's readiness to die.

In many respects, her story is reminiscent of the sacrificial asceticism of the medieval anorexic saints, who were sanctified by the Church after their deaths (Bell, 1985). These women became ascetics and embraced the path of ecstatic self-annihilation by virtue of their

intense devotion to religion, their renunciation of any earthly plea-
sures—in particular, sex, which was deemed a manifestation of the
Devil—and the consumption of the body by sacrificial practices of
all kinds. Like those medieval saints, after her sacrifice Hiba was
venerated as a heroine. Like Mohamed Atta, she went to her self-
inflicted death with an ecstatic smile on her lips; like him, she
rejected sexuality. For both, death was a longed-for goal, seen as a
state of grace or divine revelation.

L, from Chechnya, lost her father in the war when she was
twelve (Speckhard & Akhmedova, 2004). Her teacher reports that
she then immediately withdrew from other people. At school, she
was totally self-absorbed and often seemed mournful; she would
occasionally smile but never laugh. Eventually she became
extremely devout, attended the mosque, and began to wear black
Islamic robes.

This situation continued for three years until, one day, she went
to school, said goodbye to her classmates and teachers, and begged
forgiveness for everything bad she had done. Next day, together
with another girl, she drove a lorry full of explosives into the court-
yard of the Russian garrison and detonated its cargo, causing
substantial casualties among the soldiers.

It may be postulated that this young girl had failed to come to
terms with her father's death psychologically, and had therefore
deliberately sought to die. The guilt aroused by surviving her father
may have made it impossible for her to go on living. In this case,
the flight into religion must have conferred meaning on her self-
destructive decision, which thus came to belong to the experience
of mystical union with God.

Spurious vocations

Those who wish to die on account of personal problems and who
seek an external reason to underpin their decision do not succeed
in becoming suicide bombers. The terrorist act is not carried out, as
in the case described below.

Thouria Khamour was arrested at her home in Jerusalem on
suspicion of planning to blow herself up in a suicide attack. She
seemed elated by the fact of having been captured, and claimed in

an interview that she had wanted to take part in the suicide mission for personal reasons: "Sometimes a person is subjected to such great pressure and mental distress that it leads to an explosion" (Schweitzer, 2006, p. 32). She was not at all sure that she had made the right choice.

Immediately after receiving her orders, she had begun to imagine the anguish that she herself would have experienced if her own family had been destroyed in such an attack. She was also worried that God might not approve of her death and might not see her as a genuine martyr.

In a subsequent interview, Thouria gave a clearer explanation of her reasons for wanting to become a suicide martyr. At the age of twenty-five, she was still unmarried, living at home with her parents, and constantly quarrelling with them. She had already made two attempts to harm herself, but her parents had stopped her. Her worst experience had been when her father had prevented her from marrying a disabled man who loved her and whom she also loved. By standing in the way of her marriage, her father had dashed her every hope in life. Her aim in blowing herself up was to take revenge on him. For this reason, she had sought out a recruiter of candidates for suicide missions; her request had been accepted by the organization, and she had begun her training. Her preparations had been interrupted by the Israeli security service following intelligence information.

The case of Arin Ahmad, also reported by Schweitzer (2006), is similar. After being driven to the attack location with a companion, she decided at the last minute not to go ahead with her project. She had asked the driver to take her back, refusing when pressed to change her mind and to take part in the bombing after all. The other young attacker, although at first also undecided, did yield to persuasion, turned round, and completed his suicidal mission.

When captured, Arin explained that at the last minute she had had a kind of moment of truth, when she realized that the Israelis she was supposed to kill were also human beings. Their existence was not hers to dispose of, because only God had the right to decide whether people lived or died. She also explained that she had decided to become a suicide bomber because of her pain at losing the man she loved, who had been killed by the Israeli army. At first, the idea of taking revenge had not crossed her mind. She had only been aware of feeling bad and full of rage. While with a group of fellow-students at the university, she had become aware that they were planning retaliatory acts against the Israeli army. After listening to their plans in silence, one evening it had suddenly occurred to Arin that she could volunteer for a suicide mission. So she had approached the terrorist organization, which, instead of training her for several weeks in the usual way, had asked her to take part in the bombing after only four days. Arin had obeyed the attack organizer almost automatically. It was only on arrival at the chosen site that she had begun to think of the pain her death would cause her family. She added that her act was not really intended as revenge: what she in fact wanted was to send a message to the Israelis. While everyone was enjoying music, the only melody she could hear at home was the sound of shelling by Israeli tanks. She wanted the Israelis to ask themselves why on earth a Palestinian woman had blown herself up; her wish was that Israel, too, should experience the pain of the Palestinians and call its policies into question. Ultimately, however, she had been unable to go ahead with her project.

Arin aspired to suicidal martyrdom because she had been unable to work through her mourning. She had been devastated by the death of the man she loved, and the painful void left behind had made the decision to sacrifice herself virtually automatic. It had been a kind of reflex with the aim of ridding herself of pain. By killing herself and taking her enemies with her to the grave, she hoped to open a breach in the wall of insensitivity around her. She was imbued not so much with rage as with profound desolation; rather than survive, she wished to rejoin her dead lover, with whom she was totally identified. Unlike Hiba and L from Chechnya, who had banished any possibility of identification with their victims, Arin had experienced a resurgence of her human feelings at the very moment of the attack, and these had put a stop to the destructive process.

Revenge

Nasser Shawish, an al-Fatah member responsible for the training and preparation of suicide terrorists, always opposed the deployment of women for suicide missions (Schweitzer, 2006). For this reason, he tried to dissuade Abu Aisha from going ahead with her project. Aisha was a young, successful university student who could marry and have children; she could have helped her people in other ways, so why should she sacrifice herself?

To persuade her to give up her plan, Shawish had also involved his fiancée and Aisha's best friend. However, she threatened that, unless he allowed her to become a suicide martyr, she would buy a knife and kill soldiers at a roadblock, dying herself in the process. Shawish resisted the girl's pressure until, one day, his closest friend was killed and a terrorist's entire family lost their lives in an Israeli missile attack. Seeking vengeance, Shawish now acceded to Aisha's project. Another reason was that he thought her innocent appearance would be more likely to deceive the soldiers at the roadblock.

Revenge was the dominant factor for the female suicide bombers in Chechnya, too. Out of forty-nine such candidates, twenty-seven blew themselves up, three missed their target, and nineteen were killed by the Russians in the counter-terrorism operation at the Dubrovka theatre. Although this last group were killed by the Russian forces, they, too, would undeniably have detonated their explosives had it been necessary. Their determination was confirmed after the event by the testimony of family members, friends, and the hostages themselves.

For instance, a friend of one of the terrorists who died in the Dubrovka theatre was unaware of the real reason why the young attacker had travelled to Moscow: she had told her that she had gone to buy products to sell on her return to Chechnya. The friend had then asked her to buy her some boots, and wanted to give her the money, but the would-be suicide had refused it, saying they could settle when she came back. Two weeks later, when the purpose of the trip had become known, the friend found a note addressed to her in a book. It read as follows:

> I could not tell you the truth. And I could not take money from you because I could not go to paradise with unpaid debts. I know, that many people will not understand us, and will make accusations. But I believe, that you will understand all. Do not trust anything that will be said about us. They will say that we bargained and demanded dollars and a plane in exchange for the hostages. It's not the truth. We go on jihad. We know that all of us will die. We are

ready for it. We will not bargain and we will stand to the end. Forgive me if there is anything I have done to hurt you. I do not say goodbye. I know that we shall meet in heaven. Comfort my mother. She will suffer very much, she never understood me. Tell her that I myself wanted it. I am happy that I have deserved jihad. [Speckhard & Akhmedova, 2006a, p. 17]

Interviews with relatives of thirty-four Chechen suicide terrorists (twenty-six women and eight men) conducted by Speckhard and Akhmedova (2006b) reveal that none was suffering from a mental disorder, except for the traumatic consequences of experiencing or witnessing violence. Nearly all had lost family members in bombings of the civilian population, from landmines, or in "cleansing" operations by the Russian forces. Many suicide terrorists had witnessed the deaths of relations or friends from beatings and mistreatment while in prison. This had caused them great suffering, impotent rage, and a sense of guilt at having been unable to save their family members.

So it was an obvious course for them to embrace the jihadist ideology, commencing with the espousal of radical political positions and eventually leading to a willingness to take part in suicide missions. Their participation in terrorist acts was spontaneous; there is no evidence that the Chechen women were coerced by others into laying down their lives.

There is only one case on record of a woman who told the Russian authorities that she had been forced by her brother to become a suicide terrorist. In her family, split between the mother's urging her children to join the terrorist movement and the father's opposition, two sisters had already died in such missions.

According to the interviews by these two authors, the choice of suicide is favoured in Chechnya by the country's traditional shared morality of commensurate vengeance, in which the family of the victim can and must take revenge on the killer's family.

Fatima Omar Mahmoud al-Najar, aged sixty-four and a mother of nine, blew herself up a few metres from an Israeli position near a refugee camp in the Gaza Strip on 23 November 2006 (as reported in *La Repubblica*, 24 November 2006). She was probably the oldest ever female suicide bomber. She sacrificed herself with the resolute aim of revenge. Her daughter had decided to die with her, but had ultimately changed her mind at the insistence of Fatima, who wished to proceed alone. The two women's intention to die together in a suicide attack had matured gradually in their minds after the Israelis had killed one of Fatima's grandsons (her daughter's son) and wounded one of her sons, who was now confined to a wheelchair.

Their mourning was compounded by the Israeli army's shelling of Beit Hanun, in which an entire family of eighteen persons were wiped out while they slept. The two women had gone to the mosque and insisted at length on being accepted as suicide martyrs. The older woman eventually decided to embrace martyrdom alone. Wearing the clothes prepared for her, the green stripe of Hamas displayed on her forehead, and bearing a Kalashnikov, Fatima had explained the meaning of her forthcoming act on video. Then, having donned her explosive belt, she had crossed a wasteland pockmarked with mortar craters and approached an Israeli position. At a distance of a few dozen yards, the soldiers got wind of her intentions and fired at her. Fatima's bomb went off, slightly wounding three of them.

Trauma

"... memory as the thing one forgets with"

(London, 1915)

Self-annihilation

T his chapter examines the relationship between trauma and the process of dehumanization. When an individual has been exposed for too long to situations of intense emotional suffering, he may, as an extreme defence against pain, conceive a wish for self-annihilation. After all, to preserve the capacity to appreciate life, sufficiently good and stable experiences are necessary. Conversely, repeated traumatic experiences in an individual or his community disable precisely the functions that serve the continuity of existence, thus reinforcing the urge to self-destruction.

A large number of affective bonds and identity-related processes link the individual to the group. Our identity is formed and consolidated on the basis of belonging to and identifying with higher-level entities. We always need to belong to a symbolic container.

From the very beginning of life, a powerful force binds us to human objects with an attachment that remains indissoluble throughout our lives. While this bond is initially forged with our caregiver—as a rule, our mother—it progressively extends to our family and social group, our religious or political community, or our country. These objects have the function of protecting us from disorientation and the sense of solitude, and for this reason a high value is placed on them. When these containers are broken, there emerges not only pain and mourning but also catastrophic anxieties resembling those experienced in the state of helplessness and defencelessness that prevails at the beginning of life.

In the case of a massive trauma affecting an entire community and plunging it into despair, the sense of disaster overwhelms, in particular, those individuals who are more identified with the group than others and who, again more than others, become the bearers of anxiety and desolation.

The traumatic event

Trauma is a concept with many meanings, denoting a wide range of objective and subjective phenomena. The adjective "traumatic" can be applied to any violent, unforeseen event that impinges on an individual who is not yet in possession of defences adequate for protecting him from the anxiety and pain thereby aroused.

In considering the devastating psychological effects of the experience of the First World War on the combatants, Freud (1920g) used the term *trauma* in a descriptive sense, imagining the mind as enclosed in a kind of protective skin, the protective shield against stimuli, which can be penetrated or torn by a wound. In the case of a newborn or a small child, this protective-filter function is performed by the mother, with her spontaneous insight into what her child can tolerate at any given time, in accordance with his level of emotional development. If too early, the traumatic experience remains unconscious, because unrecorded, and operates in dissociation from consciousness. As we know, the capacity to remember and to be aware of a traumatic experience depends on the time of its occurrence (whether in the first months of life or later) and on its degree of violence. Certain types of emotional trauma, if experienced on a continuous basis, will inevitably alter the course of a young child's development. In some cases, the parent figures are not only unable to perform the function described by Freud of a protective filter for the infant mind, but may themselves become a source of trauma.

The various types of trauma can be visualized as extending by degrees from a total blockage of emotional development—in which case the traumatic experience is unrepresentable because its occurrence precedes the capacity to understand mental facts—to partial inhibition of emotional development, as with sexual traumas experienced in infancy.

In reviewing the histories of some of my patients, I have become increasingly aware of the importance of the sum total of adult emotional responses for mental growth. These early experiences interfere with a child's developmental potential and may result in eventual psychopathology. Even when a child has not been subjected to explicit violence, such as beating or abuse, he may sustain what could be called an *emotional trauma*, caused by the overall pattern of emotional responses from his care-giver. A trauma of this kind not only leaves "holes" in the personality, but affects its very structure, giving rise to anxieties or arrested or disturbed emotional development, with the potential result of loss of contact with the emotions.[8] This primal pathogenic configuration could be described as a *traumatic distortion of emotional experience*—that is, a set of responses by both adults and child which interfere with the child's developmental potential and may eventually result in psychopathology. This may well be the time when the nuclei that will lead to loss of emotional contact and underlie the processes of dehumanization are structured.

Destructiveness

The criterion for distinguishing between the human and the nonhuman may be said to be the emotional world—that is, the ability to form meaningful links with one's fellow human beings and to identify with them. The capacity to perceive and experience emotions—that is to say, the human condition—does not exist automatically at the beginning of life, but develops in the first relationships of care and represents a constant of psychological development. In the theories of both Freud and Klein, children are seen as greedy beings, devoted exclusively to obtaining pleasure. The transition from the paranoid-schizoid to the depressive position, as described by Klein (1946), coincides with the progressive acquisition by the infant of the perception of the mother as a separate human being who must be respected and not merely used. It is only when the depressive position is reached that the child understands that the mother is not merely an object which provides food or physical care, but possesses a separate, personal life of her own.[9] In Klein's view, this crucial transition constitutes the origin of a child's emotional life.

The sources of human destructiveness have always been the subject of vigorous debate in the psychoanalytic community. Since Freud's formulation (in 1920g) of the hypothesis of the duality of the drives, the life drive (libido) and the destructive (death) drive, psychoanalysts have been divided into two groups. The first holds that there is no such thing as a primal death drive, and that human destructiveness is always a consequence of traumatic experiences occurring in early infancy. The second, which includes Klein and her followers, invokes an innate disposition to destructiveness that is independent of environmental conditions. To avoid the destruction of the individual himself at birth, the destructive drive must be turned outward. For the primitive psyche, the enemies to be destroyed are all that oppose the maintenance of homeostasis and well-being. It is only in the course of development, and in favourable circumstances, that the individual develops an emotional world enabling him to come into contact with the emotions and feelings of others.

In clinical psychoanalysis, emotional trauma and psychopathological development are seen to be closely interwoven, thus rendering the course of therapy extremely complex. In a patient's suffering, it is often difficult to distinguish the aspects stemming from infantile trauma from those that depend on his dominant psychopathological structures.

An author who placed particular emphasis on the early interference of trauma with development was Balint (1979), the Hungarian psychoanalyst who was a pupil of Ferenczi. Balint's concept of the basic fault refers to occurrences in the earliest months of life resulting in a lack of integration in growth. The distorted mother–child relationship is incorporated early on and immediately begins to influence the infant's psychological development.

A particularly important contribution to the conceptualization of emotional trauma was made by Winnicott (1965, 1971), who stressed the dual unity of mother–child and the holding environment. Winnicott postulates the existence from birth of a potential space for development which is actualized only in the specific encounter with the mother's receptive mind.

A receptive object

According to Bion (1962, 1970), human beings are not born with an apparatus for perceiving their emotions, but have the potential to develop it. The development of this apparatus calls for a mother who gives suitable responses and confirms the child's emotional preconception.

What kind of mother is needed in order for the emotional world to develop? She must be capable from the beginning of understanding the fear, anxiety, or wish that the infant, lacking both language and thought, projects into her in order to be understood. Bion calls this action by the infant *projective identification for the purpose of communication*—the first form of communication. If the mother lacks receptive capacity, the infant is destined to be unable to understand his own sensations and needs, owing to the absence of a response that confers meaning on his projections. A child who is constantly ignored or unappreciated may eventually conceive an inner hatred of the world and a powerful wish to die.

Ferenczi must take the credit for the insight linking the death wish to emotional trauma in infancy. Given the importance of the earliest infantile experiences in strengthening or weakening the life-affirming aspects of the personality, it is understandable that a child exposed early on to psychologically unfavourable events may incorporate within himself a tendency to obliterate the vital urge. Ferenczi was the first author to consider this hypothesis. In "The unwelcome child and his death-instinct" (1929), he postulates that the lack of vitality and the wish to disappear into the void which characterize certain lives might result from the child's conscious or unconscious perception of maternal rejection. Similarly, where the conditions of dependency compel an individual to experience intolerable suffering, the wish for self-annihilation may be the response to prolonged exposure to trauma.

Rosenfeld (1978) pointed out that prolonged suffering, as in the case of a very small child who fails to receive empathic responses from the environment to his death anxieties (due for example to somatic disease involving acute physical pain), may give rise to an early nucleus of potential self-destructiveness that is likely to re-emerge in adult life. The rage and hate whose original object is the mother who is unable to help the child are inexorably targeted also at life-orientated wishes, which are felt to be responsible for unbearable suffering. (The same thing happens in the minds of trauma victims who blot out the perception of emotions lest they are thereby exposed to suffering). Anything that affirms life is perceived as a danger likely to give rise to fresh traumatic pain.

In favourable circumstances, a child who receives good enough care from the mother or the family environment begins to experience his presence in the world as meaningful. Growth processes are activated and the wish to live is manifested. However, if the individual is subjected to repeated, unbearable traumas, this equilibrium may subsequently be severely undermined and damaged: when an individual undergoes prolonged suffering in a relational desert, destructive forces directed against the self may well be reactivated.

Owing to repeated traumas, systematic attacks on human dignity, and material degradation, extermination camp inmates cease to experience emotions and become utterly indifferent to everything around them. For sheer survival, they consistently suppress any emotional impulse and blot out the living parts of themselves, so that they become mere automata. It is not by chance that the Nazi concentration camp victims, transformed as they were into dehumanized automata, were referred to as *living dead*.

Collective trauma

All large-scale traumas afflicting human communities have catastrophic consequences which, in turn, trigger chain reactions. If circumstances do not allow the members of the group to assign meaning to their experience of humiliation, to mourn for their losses, and to experience solidarity, the entire community will be pervaded by a sense of victimization and rage.

Kernberg (2003) points out that emotional traumas due to acts of collective violence have very different psychological effects from those aroused by natural disasters. By virtue of their impersonal character, the latter do not tend to give rise to hate and violence in their victims. Defeats in war, religious and racial persecution, or discrimination against minorities, on the other hand, bear the stamp of sadism and have analogous effects on the survivors.

In other words, while those affected experienced themselves as victims, at the same time they identify with the aggressor in a reversal of roles that leads to further violence. The twofold identification of victim and persecutor, fuelled by the traumatic memory, may persist for decades or even centuries, and comes to an end only when the mutual pathological projections cease and the two parties begin to glimpse the possibility of solutions other than those dictated by traumatic hate.

It may be postulated that the urge towards the destruction of life exists in latent form in all individuals, and can be activated by emotional traumas that may afflict not only the individual but also the entire community.[10] In view of the consequences of the attack on the unity and survival of the group, which are in effect attachment objects and suppliers of identity for the individual—it is readily understandable that, in territories riven by enmity and hate, the failure to take heed of collective suffering and the lack of solidarity with it give rise to a level of destructive violence that is promptly unleashed against the enemy.

As stated earlier, Volkan (2003) used the term *chosen trauma* to denote the set of traumatic experiences that have never been worked through by a community and are transmitted from generation to generation for centuries on end. One of the causes of the phenomenon of terrorism is denial of mourning and non-recognition of a people's traumatic areas. The unending wound and humiliation prevent the expression of aggressive emotions, which are transformed into homicidal destructiveness. As a general rule, the phenomenon of suicide terrorism and the counter-terrorist responses to it, which are symmetrical and often ineffective, can be regarded as a symptom of the *lack of a container for the brutal acts committed and for their non-recognition.*

Traumatized infancy

Volkan's description is borne out by the testimony of the journalists who have reported on aspects of the appalling tragedy of the Middle East.

Peter Beaumont (2003) reported in the *Observer* on the experiences of the psychologists who worked with children in the Gaza Strip, and who were unable to prevent the development of violent behaviour. They found that, up to the age of five, Palestinian children living in the refugee camps showed anxiety and fear, often exhibited language disorders, had difficulty in sleeping at night, and displayed regressive behaviour. From age six to twelve, the fear was still present, but intense hostility also began to appear. From thirteen to eighteen, hopelessness was associated with rebellious and dangerous conduct. Surprisingly, these young people felt responsible for the defeats suffered by their parents, and were convinced that it was their duty to use any means to enable the Palestinians to triumph in their struggle against Israel. A conspicuous fault line emerged between the young people and the adults: the former had no faith in peace negotiations, and saw violence as the only possible political solution. The outcome was the proliferation of a culture of death, in which young people began to see sacrifice as an ideal to be translated into reality. The parents' unworked-through trauma was re-experienced by the new generations in all its destructive magnitude.

As Peregrini (2006) writes, suicide terrorism is indeed a low-intensity war in which trauma passes from one generation to the next. The trauma experienced by the parents and their parents before them, compelled as they are to bring up their children in a climate of fear, makes the latter easy prey to defensive mental dissociations which, when amplified, underlie destructive dehumanization.

The Palestinian psychiatrist el-Sarraj, a member of the Palestinian Independent Commission for Human Rights, who was imprisoned several times by the Palestinian Authority in 1996, stated in an interview (el-Sarraj, 2004) that, according to a survey conducted in the Gaza Strip, thirty-seven per cent of children dreamt of becoming martyrs when they grew up. This proportion sends shivers down one's spine. The reason is simple: the *shahid*, in the eyes of these youngsters, is a supremely powerful figure, especially when the father figure was humiliated and effectively deprived of his role in life. After all, the martyr can be like a demigod, in that he determines whether he and others live or die. In the absence of any other positive model to idealize, children thus choose that presented by the *shahid*.

To what extent were these children manipulated by terrorist groups? The response of el-Sarraj is that they attended funerals, watched television, witnessed killings by the Israelis, and from a very early age experienced what it meant to run away from bombings and shellings. Their daily reality was pervaded by violence. If one were to ask whether hatred of the Israeli people was taught in schools, the answer might be that there was no need. All that was necessary was to grow up in a refugee camp, or not far from a Jewish settlement: any young person would wonder about the contrast between the red roofs and lovingly tilled fields of the settlement and the corrugated iron roofs, garbage heaps, and open sewers in the camp. Envy immediately arises—quite apart from the killings and torture. As a result, the Palestinians are no longer able to perceive the Israelis as human beings, but identify them with their soldiers and tanks. In just under four years of intifada, the hundred or more suicide attacks on the Israelis were mostly carried out by young people aged between eighteen and twenty-five. In some cases, would-be suicide bombers aged fourteen or fifteen were stopped.

Mohamed Mansur, a psychologist working on the Gaza Community Mental Health Programme (a project aimed at young people whose lives are blighted by war wounds), has given me a personal account of his experiences. In 1994 he and his colleagues had organized drama-based activities in Jenin with a view to helping young people to perceive and express emotions. Many of them were closed off from the world, were irritable, failed to attend classes regularly, or had difficulty at school; they passed their time in gangs throwing stones at the Israeli tanks and armoured personnel carriers. It seemed absurd for these small children to risk their lives by hurling rocks at soldiers on a war footing, who might well (and sometimes did) respond with possibly lethal bullets. Yet, this defiance had the aim of showing courage, enabling the youngsters to feel active instead of undergoing the experience of occupation passively. Risking their lives had become a thrilling sport for them. They no longer had a sense of danger, and defying death was virtually a game.

Gradually, they became interested in the theatre experience and began spontaneously to act out plots, which they themselves constructed together with the psychologists. Just one boy, Ahmed, tended to stay aloof and, if called upon to join in, confined himself to playing bit parts. For this reason, he earned the nickname of "the outsider". The psychologists subsequently learned that he had lost his parents, both of whom had been killed in an Israeli raid, and that he was being cared for by his grandparents. A few years after this experiment came to an end, the psychologists discovered that Ahmed had died in a suicide attack.

CHAPTER NINE

Dehumanization

"Praise be to God, Who created the world for His glory, Who commanded men to be just, and Who allowed the oppressed to pay back their oppressors in the same coin"

(Osama bin-Laden, in a message to al-Jazeera, March 2006)

Aggression and destructiveness

For an understanding of the specific nature of the phenomenon of terrorism, a distinction must be made between aggression, which features in every human conflict, and destructiveness. In the psychoanalytic literature from Freud on, it is not always easy to distinguish these two concepts, which sometimes appear to overlap. While aggression can be placed in the service of life when life is threatened, destructiveness is an anti-relational process that takes place in silence, is planned, and thrives in the absence of emotions. The destructive act is preceded and characterized by a subterranean process that obliterates feelings. Destructiveness is a force directed against the roots of life and the bonds that make for the survival and development of the human community. Whereas aggression is an explicit expression of rage and suffering, destructiveness presupposes the attainment of a special mental state in which feelings and emotions have been abolished. Suicide terrorism is a destructive act because it strikes at the very foundation of the bonds between human beings. It is only after destroying every human feeling that a person can die in the process of killing fellow human beings—for if emotions such as pity for the victims and for the dying self resurface in the course of a suicide attack, the destructive action is blocked. However, this occurs only in very exceptional cases.

In Carol Reed's fine film *The Third Man*, Orson Welles plays the character of Harry Lime, an unscrupulous racketeer wanted by the police in immediate post-war Vienna, then under Russian and American occupation. His old friend Holly Martins (Joseph Cotten), unaware of Harry's activities, arrives in Vienna to look him up just a few days after he has seemingly been killed in a road accident. Holly is unconvinced by the official version of events and, after many vicissitudes, finds out from certain clues that Harry is still alive, but does not know that his friend pretended to be dead so that he could operate undisturbed, without fear of detection by the police who had been hunting for him.

Concerned that his cover has been blown by Holly, Harry decides to meet him in secret; he wants to learn how much his friend knows. He intends to eliminate him before he can talk to the police. They meet at the Prater amusement park in Vienna, where, in order not to be overheard, the two men take a ride on the Big Wheel. When the carriage reaches its highest point, Harry, who has been contemplating getting rid of his friend by thrusting him out through the open door, says to him: "Look down there . . . Would you feel any pity if one of those dots stopped moving forever? . . . If I offered you £20,000 for every dot that stopped—would you really, old man, tell me to keep my money? Or would you calculate how many dots you could afford to spare?"

This memorable scene describes one of the possible versions of the process of dehumanization. This mental condition could be defined in terms of Harry Lime's statement that men are mere dots that can be eliminated. With the seduction of power and contempt for the shared values of solidarity, Lime attempts to corrupt Martins; in other words, for propaganda purposes he uses the same arguments that seduced his own mind. He is here expressing a cynical, perverse attitude in which empathy with the fate of others is totally lacking.[11]

Emotional indifference

Nowadays, achievement of the mental state of emotional indifference that underlies the process of dehumanization is facilitated by the use of technology, which enables a person to kill without the perception of killing.

> They are so remote from their so-called enemies, and they have to aim from such a distance, that they are no longer really *aiming;* they no longer have any perception of their victims, they have no knowledge of them, and cannot even imagine them. Not before, not while it is happening, and not afterwards. Can such things be called *soldiers?* And how could such soldiers hate people they have never met and (considering that they will have been eliminated) never will meet? Moreover, these soldiers, who no longer engage in hand-to-hand combat, who no longer share a battlefield with the enemy, but are at best manipulating instruments in some ill-defined place from which not a single enemy soldier is within sight—why would these soldiers need hate? Is it not, would it not be, an utterly superfluous feeling? One that is absolutely outdated? [p. 63]

This long quotation is taken from an essay whose title translates as "The outdatedness of hating" by the philosopher Günther Anders (1985),[12] an author who always spoke out against war and the destructiveness of man, and who drew particular attention to the danger of dehumanization that is characteristic of our age.

War, too, is characterized by dehumanization. Whereas hate directed at another person is inherent in humanity, that is to say, it is a human feeling, the danger of dehumanization lies precisely in indifference, in the absence of emotions. Man's emotional apparatus, Anders continues, does not possess a natural, immutable character, but may be destined to decay and indeed to disappear. In our age, even hate, which, after all, has always led to war and destruction, runs the risk of seeming outdated:

> In the good old days, soldiers threatened and massacred each other, and wars were fought by men capable of hatred! So they were

human beings. And those who hated each other might one day, in certain circumstances, also cease to hate; and thus cease to fight; and cease to exterminate; or perhaps even begin to love each other. [p. 58]

Again:

Bombs and missiles do not have eyes that can tell uniforms apart from other garments. The reality of equality today is that any civilian has the same right to be killed as a member of the armed forces ... For the active participants, everything is identical; everything is identical in value; everything is indifferent; and everything is identical in its absence of value: their act is absolute indifference, nihilism in action. [Anders, 2006, p. 54]

Even if acts of war often affect the civilian population, for the military personnel who carry them out, little significance seems to attach to the killing of helpless civilians. For the suicide bomber, too, the problem of the suffering he will inflict on innocent victims does not arise. His experience is more complex because the dehumanizing process has extended to his own person, so that he sees even himself as a mere *dot* that can easily be blotted out. Blowing up a bus full of unsuspecting passengers or attacking a disco full of young people is indicative of the loss of any emotional sense for life. Total indifference to one's own life and the lives of others, as in suicide terrorism, is the extreme expression of dehumanization.

Said fails to go through with his first attempt at a suicide mission because he is not completely *dehumanized*: the sight of an unwitting child in the bus he is about to blow up arouses an emotion in him which blocks his destructive intent. Because he has not yet entirely lost the capacity to empathize with others, he cannot help identifying emotionally with the child.

Akhtar (2003) points out that the dehumanization characteristic of the phenomenon of terrorism differs from that observed in certain pathological processes—for instance, in children who grow up without any experience of human relations, in psychotic or congenital mental disorders, or in identification with cruel figures as in the case of serial killers. As we have seen, the dehumanization implicit in the destructiveness of the terrorist also differs from that manifested in murder–suicide, where the perpetrator's motives are personal and which is attributable to passion-driven violence. In suicide terrorism, any personal motivation—and the choice is often in fact dictated by repeated emotional trauma—must rid itself of subjective emotion in order to become an impersonal act. Since politics is governed by the impersonal logic of power, the sacrifice of the suicide terrorist too must remain in the impersonal register.

CHAPTER TEN

Dissociating emotions

"Eight years ago, I helped to make a television series that tried to explain why so many Muslims had come to hate the West. Last night, I remembered some of those Muslims in that film, their families burnt by American-made bombs and weapons. They talked about how no one would help them but God. Theology versus technology, the suicide bomber against the nuclear power. Now we have learnt what this means"

(Fisk, 2005, p. 1031)

Escape from pain

Many terrorists-to-be have grown up in a daily climate of abuse and violence and developed depressive reactions. Some have lost their jobs and had to survive by living on their wits amid a succession of humiliations. A high proportion of the traumatized population will never become terrorists, let alone suicide bombers, but a small group will be attracted by this solution.

Speckhard (2006) uses the concept of *dissociation* to explain the mental state of the suicide bomber. Her starting point is the definition of the phenomenon of dissociation given in the American Psychiatric Association's *Diagnostic and Statistical Manual of Mental Disorders* (*DSM-IV*), which defines dissociation as a disruption in the usually integrated functions of consciousness, memory, identity, or perception of the environment. In suicide terrorists, an emotional barrier, or dissociation, prevents perception of the anxiety that would otherwise be aroused by the decision to take their own lives and to kill. In some cases this split is so severe that the event of death is encapsulated, so that it is isolated from the normal activities of daily life. The author mentions the case of an aspiring suicide who had planned to die in an attack after taking his final university examinations. This example shows that the reality of death can be split off from the rest of life. Dissociation is stated to be a defence deployed by persons whose survival is under constant threat and who can no longer tolerate any further suffering. Some traumatized young people ultimately deaden their emotions completely; they feel so emotionally stupefied that they describe themselves as "already dead". It is precisely these subjects who are ideal candidates for suicide missions.

This capacity for emotional "stupefaction" due to continual emotional traumas may explain why death is not experienced as an event that arouses anxiety, but instead often gives rise to a state of excitement and pleasure.

According to the testimony of the Dubrovka theatre hostages (Speckhard & Ahkmedova, 2004), the attackers were in a euphoric mental state. A doctor present at the scene reports that, after the terrorists had surrounded the theatre and set their bombs, all the women in the group seemed to be in a strange condition of euphoria, except for one who seemed afraid. This observation is borne out by witness reports of the apparent state of grace possessing the minds of suicide terrorists in Palestine and Iraq. Suffering, pain, and impotence transform the spirit of the suicide-to-be, crushing his emotions, and with them the survival instinct itself. In this situation, death itself becomes a relief, an escape from the subject's pain.

Zacharia Zubeidi, a member of the al-Aqsa Martyrs' Brigades responsible for training volunteers for suicide missions, notes that suicide martyrs lose their flexibility of thought (Speckhard, 2005). All the cells in their minds seem to be dead except for one which suggests that death is a liberation. Zacharia himself admits that, having experienced devastation and the senseless deaths of some of his companions, he too tends to lapse into the same state of passivity and resignation, and feels the desire to embrace death immediately. However, in his case this mental state lasts for only a short time, just one or two hours, whereas the suicide-to-be never emerges from it and goes to his death in this condition.

When human feelings are subjected to excessive stress, they must be expelled and destroyed. In this way, dissociation obliterates any emotional perception, and with it any empathy and human pity for the bomber's own dying self and the other unfortunates who meet their end through his act.

Death as liberation

A traumatized individual does not wish to go on living; surviving those dear to him gives rise to a sense of guilt. The affects and love objects that maintain personal identity and confer meaning on life have been utterly destroyed, and the future does not exist. For the aspiring suicide bomber, surviving and keeping the affective parts of himself alive is tantamount to exposing himself to new pain and torment. By blowing himself up, the martyr not only kills the enemy responsible for the suffering, but also eliminates the living parts of himself that are compelled to survive in agony. The constriction of the mind—a virtual emotional stupor—observed by many students of the phenomenon in would-be terrorists betokens an affective felo de se that precedes the destruction of their own body.

Suicide terrorism is the end result of a combination of specific social dynamics and personal motivations. It could not exist without the exaltation of sacrificial death in their community, which, while shared by all its members, makes converts in particular among the young people who agree to lay down their lives in order to be idealized by the community. They are beset, entrapped, and seduced by a chorus of propaganda in posters, songs, and videos.

For some youngsters, the alternative to suicide martyrdom might be the dynamic of murder–suicide. Some Palestinians have approached Israeli settlements armed with guns and explosives, attempting to kill as many people as possible before themselves dying in the process. In this case, the suicidal act is experienced actively. This is not the case with human bombs. Rather than killing, they sacrifice themselves first, and destroy second. They do not belong to the military organization, but are volunteers for death—latter-day Samsons who wish to take as many Philistines as possible with them to the grave.

On very rare occasions only, a sudden thought or memory succeeds in reactivating the emotional circuit, thus disrupting the process of destructive triumph. However, where trauma has led to irreversible emotional death, and where destructive rage has become the sole reason for the act and deadened every emotion, it is much more difficult to defuse the destructive potential. The sense of humanity can no longer be recovered when it has been left too far behind and the subject is convinced that he is acting in the name of a God on high.

CHAPTER ELEVEN

Unique identity and omnipotence

"What kind of bird are you if you can't fly ?" twittered the
little bird. "And what kind of bird are you," retorted the
duck, "when you can't even swim?"

(Prokofiev, *Peter and the Wolf*)

Difference

Racism of all kinds, whether or not it extends to genocide, as
in the case of Nazism or, more recently, in Rwanda, is
fuelled by insistent propaganda that denigrates those who
are different, who do not belong to the dominant group. In this way,
even persons who could not individually lay claim to elevated
status in society feel superior, seeing themselves as the bearers of
absolute values. In accordance with this presumed supremacy,
political propaganda endorses the right to destroy those who are
"different". To legitimize their oppression and to justify the
massacre of the victims, the aggressors often construct a myth of
past victimization.

As Sen (2006, p. xiv) points out, in the age of globalization the phenomenon of unique identity is particularly worrying because it underlies many of the conflicts and atrocities in the world:

> The uniquely partitioned world is much more divisive than the universe of plural and diverse categories in which we live. It goes not only against the old-fashioned belief that "we human beings are all much the same" . . . but also against the less discussed but much more plausible understanding that we are *diversely different*.

The propaganda that preaches the idea of unique identity is fuelled by the conditions in which many individuals live, conforming and submitting to the appointed authority. These characteristics are not confined to technologically backward communities. Many complex societies have been unable to respond to human problems, which are sacrificed on the altar of conformism or competition. The drive to excel (in school, at work, or in society) may pave the way for a kind of false growth or an adhesive identity that stands in the way of genuine autonomy. Under pressure of this kind, people may conform to prevailing opinions, and the capacity of the individual to think creatively and originally will be crippled. Later in his book, Sen writes (*ibid.*, p. 175):

> It is not remarkable that generating the illusion of unique identity, exploitable for the purpose of confrontation, would appeal to those who are in the business of fomenting violence, and there is no mystery in the fact that such reductionism is sought. But there is a big question about why the cultivation of singularity is so successful, given the extraordinary naïveté of that thesis in a world of obviously plural affiliations.

The utopia of a unique identity makes conflict between peoples inevitable. The "globalized" world involves a contest between two different types of idealization: on the one hand, the Western lifestyle, which is democratic and technocratic; and, on the other, that of Islam, which seeks to maintain tradition and hierarchy against the paganism of globalized modernity. This idealization is based on a radical split between good and bad, involving the perception of the other, the "different", as inferior, diseased, or positively diabolical. If we are in possession of everything good, the different must be combated and destroyed because it is dangerous.

Klein (1946) called a mental condition of this kind the *paranoid–schizoid position*, a perception of the other as bad and dangerous so that it must be combated in order to preserve the subject's own self. The assertion of a unique identity entails a process of falsification. Psychic reality—that is, the set of beliefs that underlie the perception of oneself and others—is never unique and immutable. Its origins lie in the overall complex of subjective experiences, which evolve in time and space. A group that claims to be the bearer of a unique reality, on the other hand, aspires to manufacture a unique identity in order to eliminate the multiplicity of experiences, cultures, and traditions that are the heritage of all mankind.

Wherever a unique identity is proclaimed, it is highly probable that a subgroup endowed with political power is claiming to speak for all. This is the approach to the wielding of power espoused by the dictatorships that have caused so much bloodshed throughout the world, both in past centuries and in recent times.

The idealization that leads to the notion of unique identity uses a propaganda of falsification that corrupts the truth. For narcissism afflicts not only the individual but also entire peoples: at collective level too, we may see ourselves as superior and those who are different from us as inferior.

Conversely, a space open to the reception of emotions and human relations allows the other to be experienced as a meaningful enrichment to our existence. In other words, we are confronted with the difficult task of keeping our minds open to emotions in all their complexity, rather than deadening them in ideological simplification.[13]

Sharing emotions

Neuroscientific research bears out certain well-established insights by psychoanalysts, who are in constant contact with the human mind. A topical issue in the neurosciences is the way in which human minds perceive each other and how feelings are transmitted between individuals: the human capacity to communicate one's emotions allows one's interlocutor to share in one's experience for himself, without thereby ceasing to be separate. It is only in this way that an individual can respond empathically to another and come to his aid. This is a sign of mental health, which is the complete opposite of the phenomena of indifference and alienness whereby the other is seen as an enemy who does not belong to one's own world.

Rizzolatti & Gallese (1998) discovered the existence of so-called *mirror neurons*, a group of nerve cells that are activated when we see another human being performing an action involving movement. In other words, certain groups of cells begin to resonate, and activate the same muscles as those used at the time by someone performing a specific purposive action. This activation is not equivalent to the triggering of an *imitative process*, but instead tends to establish sensorimotor procedures that are learned unconsciously in early life: their unconscious repetition facilitates access to a motor alphabet that provides the subject with a better understanding of the intentions of the person performing the relevant action. In a word, we ourselves are the mirror, and the sensorimotor neurons permit the activation of a complex, pre-formed system whose function is to facilitate communication with others.

The same mechanism, based on the capacity to internalize and reproduce what is perceived in the other, may perhaps also underlie the ways in which the individual learns to apprehend not only the meaning of other people's actions, but also their sensations or emotions. However, to understand another person's mental state, imitative procedures do not suffice; what is required is the possession of an emotional world—that is, a disposition of the mind in contact with internalized human relations. The understanding of others is impossible in the absence of such an internal world.

However, what underlies the construction of this place in the mind that enables us to understand others emotionally? In my view, we can understand our fellow human beings only if we have, in turn, been understood and have fully internalized the experience of emotional contact with others. In order to be born and to develop as individuals, we must have been received emotionally in the mind of an adult (primordially, the mother's mind). The processes of humanization have their origins in this primitive, inescapable fact. Without the specific experience of being understood, we cannot introject that same function, which is a prerequisite of emotional communication with others. In such a case, the *emotional mind* fails to develop. A child deprived of emotional reception may develop every cognitive, logical, or performative skill, but will lack the possibility of an internalized relational life.

Yet it is insufficient to assert that all that is necessary for the acquisition of a sense of identity is to have been received in someone's mind; the manner in which this process takes place must also be considered.

When an infant seeks recognition from his mother, what does her response give back to him? The quality of the parental response can help the child to gain a realistic perception of himself, which will either enable him to relate to the world or, possibly, impel him to deny the truth, thus making for a grandiose, narcissistic identity. This may happen if the mother sees her child as an exceptional being and causes him to believe that he is a special person, destined to become master of the world. Such a situation reinforces the notion of grandiosity, legitimizing the expectation of privilege and an attitude of arrogance and high-handedness. The eventual adult will remain in the paranoid-schizoid position and see anyone who threatens his presumed superiority as an enemy.

Silent messages pass constantly from one generation to the next. The manner in which we treat the other, the "alien", may also be transmitted unconsciously by adults. In addition, we introject our parents' anxieties and fears; for this reason, if we have lived in a family or social environment pervaded by fear and persecution, we shall carry with us this mental disposition towards those who are different, and shall be inclined to regard them as potential enemies.

Omnipotence and destructiveness

Let us now return to the problem of trauma and the processes of dehumanization. Can a causative connection be established between emotional trauma and the dehumanizing process? Is the tendency to destructive behaviour always linked to trauma? These questions must be answered if an overall view of the complex phenomenon of suicide terrorism is to be gained.

There are two possible ways of conceiving the phenomenon of terrorism. On the one hand, it can be regarded as the expression of a diabolical part of humanity—an envious and destructive part that is mobilized against the democracy and prosperity of the *civilized*

(Western) part; or, on the other, it may be regarded as a violent reaction to the invasive presence of a military and technological power incapable of respecting the values of other cultures and societies.

In this connection, it may be helpful briefly to consider again the clinical situation in psychoanalysis. With regard to the problems arising in the therapy of difficult patients who are seemingly not amenable to psychoanalysis (De Masi, 2002, 2006), my attempts to establish a link between severe forms of psychopathology and infantile trauma have had extremely uncertain results. While acknowledging the role of infantile emotional trauma in the generation of adult suffering, I am convinced that, in most cases of serious pathology, it is not easy to find evidence of violent, repeated traumas in infancy. Instead, the common factor in pathology of this kind is mental absence on the part of the parents—that is, parental indifference to the child's emotional development. This emotional remoteness allows the infant, from the earliest months of life, to flee from psychic reality and take refuge in pathological withdrawal (whether megalomaniacal, fantasy-based, or sexualized). Pathological identifications with grandiose characters, who are felt to be providers of pleasure, take shape in this psychic withdrawal, together with progressive abandonment of the world of relationships.

In my view, two equally important and mutually potentiating factors tend to facilitate the distortion of growth. A synergy exists between lack of empathy from the environment and the construction by the infant of psychopathological structures that steer him away from normal development. In other words, infantile traumas do not bear the sole responsibility for the adult's suffering and psychopathology.

In a famous book by Miller (1980), this prolific Swiss psychoanalytic author considered why the children of violent and abusive parents grow up to ill-treat others. An unloved or unwanted child has the potential to become a violent adult who will take revenge on others for the traumas to which he was subjected, or who will beat his own children so that they ultimately become robots that can simply be made use of, thus quite possibly creating a future generation of oppressors or criminals. Miller holds that a child's aggression is positive, necessary for his survival, and derived from the life instinct. In her view, it is events subsequent to birth that cause the psyche to develop in a negative direction. In a traumatic environment, feelings must be suppressed and aggressors idealized, so that in this situation a child will grow up without any awareness of what was done to him. The now split-off feelings of anger, powerlessness, and despair will continue to find expression in destructive acts against others (criminality) or the subject himself (drug or alcohol addiction, prostitution, mental disorders, or suicide).

In her passionate defence of the ill-treated child, this author also examines the case of Adolf Hitler, who, as a child, was constantly beaten by his father. The German dictator's traumatic infancy is adduced as a partial explanation for the destructive character of his political leadership. In my opinion, however, Miller fails adequately to stress the fact that, besides the conflict with his father, Hitler enjoyed the boundless admiration of his mother (and later his sister), so that this maternal exaltation may have helped to convince him that he was a superman justified in destroying the Jewish enemies and crushing other nations to facilitate the triumph of greater Germany. However, rather than attempting a pathography of Hitler, I merely wish to point out here that the relationship between trauma and the process of dehumanization is not always entirely straightforward.

Trauma is not solely responsible for human destructiveness; a more important part may well be played by the allure of grandiose figures who give rise to confusion between good and bad. In such a case, part of the personality justifies destructive behaviour in the name of a moral imperative. Certain forms of international terrorism, inspired by religious fundamentalism, cannot be explained on the basis of trauma, but only by an analysis of their grandiose pathology. They involve the subordination of the individual (and the community) to a value system stemming from a perversion of conscience. This is the psychological condition embodied in Harry Lime, the protagonist of *The Third Man*, discussed in Chapter Nine.

Destructive narcissism

Rosenfeld (1971) and Meltzer (1973) suggest that the origins of severe psychopathologies lie in a mental structure which, through seductive propaganda, overcomes and colonizes the healthy parts of the personality and compels them to espouse destructiveness. The power of this nucleus is exercised with spurious promises of happiness or threats of punishment. This pathological structure, to which severe forms of mental suffering are attributed, has been called *destructive narcissism* or the *psychotic part of the personality*. The most insidious element in this mental state is the lack of a clear consciousness of its pathological objectives, which may actually be seen as inevitable, positive aspirations. In such a case, the drive towards pathological behaviour operates in secrecy and silence; these patients' personalities are seemingly dominated by a deadly force that presents itself as possessing idealized, exciting, and positive characteristics.

This model facilitates understanding of the way in which individual and collective components come together in the phenomenon of suicide terrorism. It may be postulated that the ethic of sacrifice that finds expression in the leaders' political vision comes into being as the pathological part of the system that captivates many other minds and impels them in the direction of destructive suicide. It is not difficult to guess at the kind of promises and expectations, whether earthly or ideal, that are held out to the young terrorists-to-be, and at the secretly nurtured fantasies that distance them from all affective bonds (with their children, wives, community, and so on). In this way, individual omnipotent fantasies combine with seductive political propaganda.

A prerequisite of the phenomenon of suicide terrorism is the meeting and *synergic action of these two components—the network (the psychotic part) and the willing compliance of the individual*—with the terrorist's impotent rage and wish for martyrdom and ideal sacrifice. As with the structures observed in severe psychopathologies, in this phenomenon too one is astonished at the passivity and docility with which the healthy part of the personality allows itself to be dominated by the destructive nucleus.

A possible reason why some individuals exhibit such *docility* in embracing self-annihilation is afforded by certain observations on the phenomena that accompany the dissolution of personal identity. Whereas the prospect of separating from life usually gives rise to anxiety and depression, in some cases this abandonment is experienced as liberating or even as positively ecstatic. This state may be attained by appropriate strategies, such as deep meditation, mystical trance states, or perverse techniques. In masochistic practices (De Masi, 1999) and pathological processes, a person may achieve *over-sensual* experiences (as Sacher-Masoch called them). This would explain how death can be courted in a state of pleasurable excitement.

The escalation of the terrorist act is similar in some respects to that of perverse activity: it stems not only from the necessity of revenge, but also from factors inherent in the nature and dynamics of destructive triumph.

To keep up the level of excitement, the doses of "badness" must be constantly increased in perverse acts too. A literary demonstration of this situation can be found in Sade's *The One Hundred and Twenty Days of Sodom and Other Writings* (1784). Just when the libertines have their victims totally at their disposal and can do whatever they want with them—and even take their lives—the problem of habituation to excitement arises. They realize that, even if they constantly raise the level of violence, they will never be satisfied, and that no act of wickedness can ever fulfil the aspirations in their minds. The real crime, rather than a series of wretched misdeeds, would be to destroy the sun in order to abolish the universe.

The grandiose element of some terrorist attacks also recalls the situation sometimes observed in the suicide of melancholics. Two inseparable processes—hatred of life and revenge on humanity—are involved in both melancholic and terrorist suicides; hence the spectacular nature of some of the former. The desire to exact exemplary revenge and to amplify the attack on life explains why some individuals kill themselves by plunging from monuments or famous landmarks rather than ending their lives quietly. The destructive act must be celebrated in ostentation and grandiosity, and the subject's corpse must be cast before the world.

In the case of terrorism, the choice of a grandiose target (such as the Twin Towers in New York) may possibly stem not only from the need to attack the symbols of the enemy's power and to terrify the population, but also from the wish for spectacular vengeance. From this point of view, every suicide bombing aspires to a grandiose setting. The revenge aspect of a terrorist act is fulfilled more in the spectacular image of an aircraft exploding in flight than in an attack on some other target that might be equally rewarding. The grandiosity of the event—attributable not only to the number of victims—is a source of fascination for those who conceive and perpetrate it. Pleasure is raised to a high pitch of exaltation in grandiose destruction.

CHAPTER TWELVE

A cannibal God

"It seems to me that the gods exist only in the human brain,
and that they thrive or decay in the self-same universe that
invented them"

(José Saramago, from an article in *El País*,
18 September 2001, translated)

The God of enmity

What can the religious solution offer a person in the throes of a profound traumatic crisis? To someone who feels disorientated, anxious, and deprived of a country of his own, joining a religious community holds out the prospect of reconstituting his identity. While a fundamentalist religious community performs this protective function, at the same time it demands total adherence to its creed. Many of those who will eventually become human bombs begin to attend the mosque regularly, give up their routine activities, and distance themselves from their social and family group. Their outward appearance also changes: men grow beards, while women wear the traditional black robe and veil.

These individuals speak enthusiastically about jihad, the duties of the believer, purity, and the possibility of going to Paradise; and they encourage their family and friends to make the same choice. Many converts separate from spouses and friends who do not share their convictions.

This journey of spiritual transformation inevitably puts one in mind of the religious faith that inspired the lives of many saints in certain dark periods of Western history (Bell, 1985). For them too, renunciation and suffering were the price to be paid in exchange for mystical union with God and ascent to Paradise. However, the ethic of purity and sacrifice at the same time opened the way to the destruction of life.

Any religious system harbours dangers when it aspires to uniqueness and the imposition of its beliefs on others by means of violence. Once its priests project hatred of the enemy on to him, God is transformed into an omnipotent vehicle of enmity and rancour. This is exemplified by the representation of God used in terrorist political propaganda. It is the image of God itself that has been transformed: he is not only a cruel God, but also one who is vengeful and demands human sacrifices. The Old Testament God too demanded human sacrifice in order to be appeased. To obtain forgiveness, the believer, Abraham, had to sacrifice something precious and dear to him (his son Isaac).

The God of the fundamentalists insists on human sacrifice not in order to forgive the transgressions of the faithful, but, being narcissistically hypersensitive and full of hate, with the aim of taking revenge on the enemy. He is like a feudal lord enjoying the total subjugation of his vassals, who must lay down their lives if only to protect him from harm.

The God of Abraham insisted on observance of the primitive law and established himself as the arbiter of its transmission from generation to generation. The God of the Islamic fundamentalists, on the other hand, seduces his followers by eliminating everything human in them as well as any consideration for life; in demanding submission and the extreme sacrifice from the believer, this God reveals his true perverse, cruel nature.

In the *fundamentalist religious variant*, divine intransigence privileges only those who appease God's fury. To approach his God, a believer must first of all become pure, abandon earthly needs, and eventually give up even the wish to live. This God does not aspire to convert other potential believers to his creed; nor does he wish to redeem the faithful by re-establishing the Law. He is not like the severe but just God of Abraham; instead, in order to achieve his aim, he seduces his followers by promising eternal bliss in exchange for their lives. To be certain of eternal salvation, the believer is driven to crime without the awareness of guilt.

This, to my mind, is an important point. Where violence is acted out in the name of the community or religion, the sense of guilt accompanying any destructive act can be avoided. For this reason, the aspiring suicide seeks legitimization of his choice in the religious organization. That choice is not the will of the individual, but the command of God. Killing at God's behest will legitimize the massacre. Indeed, this God compensates the individual for his sacrifice by offering him the joys of Paradise: a state of well-being and pleasure awaits the terrorist as soon as he has rid himself of his mortal body.

What kind of *morality*, then, is inherent in this divine figure? God, as the ideal object of fundamentalism, is the representative of a moral practice based on submission and on the veneration of savagery and revenge. Since morality has been perverted by cruelty, the nature of this God is deadly. The greater the desperation of the community, the more powerful the new Godhead becomes in the minds of the faithful. The idol who demands human sacrifices is not seeking a solution to the community's plight, but instead suggesting responses that perpetuate the trauma.

A perverse system

It is a well-known fact that every perverse system presents itself as a hyper-moral organization. That, in my view, is the most salient feature of the terrorist variant of fundamentalism. In this vision, *morality* is equivalent to a perverse system. Indeed, one may wonder whether the use of the term "religion" is legitimate where faith coincides with destructiveness practised in the name of religion.

Other political organizations have employed suicide terrorism without invoking a religious motivation. Militant groups with no particular allegiance to a specific faith, such as the PKK in Turkey or the Tamil Tigers in Sri Lanka, have used it, justifying its choice as a rational and effective instrument of struggle through tactical or political arguments.

On the subjective level, however, one factor makes religious faith useful for the purpose of terrorist martyrdom. The ecstatic state of mind that can be achieved by religious self-hypnosis plays a part in containing death anxiety and facilitates the act of suicide. Stein (2002) points out that the obsessive observance of religious rules and the repetition of ritualized prayers can help the terrorist to overcome fear, while reinforcing the dissociative trance state necessary for his mission when it is carried out. This explains the condition of bliss with which many terrorists go to their deaths. The act of self-annihilation is tantamount to abandoning life forever in a state of glorious union with God.

When an aspiring suicide joins the religious group, this is obviously the conclusion of a journey—the culmination of a drama begun much earlier. The espousal of a religion is an extreme solution to a personal tension that could not be resolved in any other way. The religious group constitutes the *network* that comes together with the individual destructive project that has been maturing in silence. An individual who feels abandoned by all but himself will seek to withdraw into closed-off, sectarian spaces in order to find reasons—partly imaginary and partly real—for revenge. One of these refuges may be the fundamentalist religious organization, which imposes its vision of struggle in competition with other political groups to which the use of suicide martyrs is alien. In this situation, the fundamentalist position becomes particularly attractive to someone who sees personal sacrifice as a unique retaliatory weapon and a way out of despair.

While some Islamic religious groups admittedly accept suicide martyrdom, the position of some governments, reinforced by the Western media, that suicide terrorism is attributable almost exclusively to the religious factor is in some respects misleading. This interpretation ignores the fact that the phenomenon has its origins in complex and severe sociopolitical problems. Such a view risks diverting public attention on to factors that are not of primary importance for an understanding of suicide terrorism.

Believers in Islam differ among themselves in many respects—in their political and social values, their philosophy, and their attitudes to the West. Espousal of fundamentalist ideology does not coincide with the intensity with which individual believers practise their faith; many Muslims, while extremely devout, firmly believe in the need for peaceful coexistence among nations.

A vision identifying Islam exclusively with the Koran and its prophetic tradition has manifestly come to dominate the Western conception of that religion. However, whatever one might think or read, fundamentalism, far from stemming from Islamic tradition, is in fact a product of the modern world (Allam, 2006). It is based on a financing and recruitment network to which any national logic is alien. Its very cultural basis is a by-product of the individualism that permeates the societies whose enemy it claims to be.

CHAPTER THIRTEEN

Terrorism: reversible or irreversible?

"Wherever morality is based on theology, wherever the right is made dependent on divine authority, the most immoral, unjust, infamous things can be justified and established"

(Feuerbach, 1989)

Two types of terrorism

W hile suicide terrorism is generally thought of as homogeneous in nature, I shall attempt in this chapter to distinguish some particular features of this phenomenon on the basis of which two broad categories with different political aims and personal motivations can be identified.

Nationalist terrorism

The first form of organization to be considered is that of localized, nationalist terrorism, whose origins lie in the traumatic circumstances of an oppressed community. In this context, a political group is established which, in addition to traditional methods of struggle, eventually decides to use the weapon of suicide terrorism, in the knowledge that the psychological conditions exist for certain individuals to present themselves spontaneously for such missions. A possible example is that of Palestinian suicide terrorism, which some young people have seen as the offering of blood necessary for the foundation of their nation.

The ill-being that paved the way for terrorism of this kind was psychological and emotional in nature. In the daily lives of the Palestinian population, humiliation and the undermining of dignity were accompanied by the subversion of roles and the enfeeblement of community solidarity. For Palestinian youngsters forced to live in impoverished neighbourhoods, oppressed by the daily presence of the Israeli army, and confronted with the prosperity of the occupying settlers, the prospects of a secure life had become virtually non-existent. Given these mental and environmental conditions, martyrdom seemed to be a way out of all the moral wretchedness in which other Palestinians had to live, alongside the black market, petty theft and, on occasion, collaboration with the Israeli intelligence service. Having previously felt inferior and despised, martyrdom candidates derived a sense of "superiority" from the fear they inspired and the pride they manifested. Khosrokhavar (2003) uses the term *martyropathy* to denote the choice made by these young Palestinians, with the aim not of winning a battle, but of laying down their lives in order to justify their rejection of a world that had become impossible to live in. Indeed, the radical choice of martyrdom also entailed the withdrawal of legitimacy from the Palestinian government, which, with its corruption and authoritarianism, was seen as standing in the way of the people's participation in the construction of a society of their own.

In the nationalist type of terrorism, such as that of Palestine, martyrs sought to present their sacrifice as the only possible way of reversing the failure of the struggle for liberation; their desperate act became the expression of a situation of mourning that could not be worked through. Terrorism of this kind can be regarded as *reversible*, because it is plausible to assume that this strategy can be abandoned if and when the social and political conditions that inspired it change.

Again, an individual aspiring suicide might change his mind about volunteering for a mission if he were to glimpse the possibility of a different form of struggle to facilitate the achievement of his aims. In other words, the need for reparation, which has paradoxically underlain the suicidal choice of many young people, can find forms of expression other than the deliberate sacrifice of their lives. An appropriate political response is capable of motivating an individual fighter to leave the extremist organization, which, by its nature, is unable to accept a policy of compromise. For this reason, to discourage the vocation of martyrdom and spontaneous enlistment in the terrorist network, it is vital to reduce the level of trauma in the community.

Fundamentalist terrorism

A second form of terrorism, which in my opinion *is not reducible*, has its origins in a grandiose, totalitarian design. An example is that practised by *al-Qaeda*, whose destructive potential rests on the grandiosity of its leaders, with their dream of establishing a worldwide Muslim community after the destruction of the empire of evil—that is to say, the West, as embodied by the USA, as well as, to a lesser extent, by other Western societies.

I have already mentioned the dynamic of revenge demanded by wounded narcissism. The most intransigent and violent reactions are indeed observed when trauma impinges on subjects living in a state of paranoid omnipotence.[14] The phenomenon of the Japanese kamikaze cannot be understood except in the context of their idealized fusion with the figure of the emperor, the omnipotent father. In a fundamentalist organization too, the leader is idealized as the interpreter of the divine will. The fundamentalist ideology is puritanical, sets no store by individual emotional life, and takes on an anti-sexual character (Kernberg, 2003). From this point of view, the individual is placed in the service of a purifying mythology. The leadership of these groups is often assumed by persons with an elite background, who are, nevertheless, idolized by the traumatized masses.

A huge gulf separates a Palestinian seeking the establishment of a nation, a Chechen demanding independence from Russia, a Bosnian compelled to fight in order to avoid annihilation by the

Serbian army, a Tamil fighter claiming part of the territory occupied by government forces, and an al-Qaeda member who vows to destroy not only imperialism but also every form of Western culture. Although operational links have existed between the two types of terrorism, their aims are different: the former is realistic and feasible, while the latter is ideological and unachievable. The objective of ideological terrorism is indeed omnipotent, because it presupposes the collapse of the very organization on which the world rests, this world being neither Western nor corrupt, but complex and diverse. The terrorists themselves belong to it and have learned its methods. The enrolment of terrorists in networks such as Osama bin-Laden's can be understood only in terms of the intense hatred of fairly small groups of radicalized Muslims for a Western world seen as a global enemy. These Westernized Muslims nurture the myth of the purity and unity of the earliest Islamic communities, which are even portrayed as having existed in a golden age.

The distinction I wish to make is between *secular* terrorism, whose demands are political and which is, therefore, potentially reversible, and *religious* terrorism, which is irreducible because its action is seen as inspired by the supreme will of the Godhead. The difference is, in my view, important because it can help us to avoid confusing two phenomena that call for different political responses to, and different interpretations of, the motivations of individual attackers.

Mohamed Atta and his companions had never been exposed to traumatic experiences or political repression: the majority of the suicide attackers involved in the terrorist missions in the USA came from the Arabian Peninsula and from countries not under foreign occupation. Although mostly Arabs, the members of al-Qaeda belong to different communities and are united only by the common objective of destroying the West and its values. The aspiring suicides' quest for Paradise then becomes subservient to their leaders' political dream of imposing their hegemony in *this world*.

Pain and suffering at a distance

To return to the subject of fundamentalist terrorism, it is not easy to understand how it developed. I shall confine myself here to mentioning some of the views expressed at a meeting on terrorism held by the British Psychoanalytical Society in London in 2002 (a commentary (in Italian) on this meeting can be found in Lussana (2002)). The conclusions are similar to those of other psychoanalysts (Varvin & Volkan, 2003) and of those political commentators who have attempted also to understand the other side's point of view. Marco Chiesa (2002) points out in his contribution that the political elites and the public at large are indifferent to catastrophes affecting faraway peoples. For example, hardly anyone has drawn adequate attention to the tragedy that unfolded in Iraq after the Anglo-American intervention. The Gulf War, in which thousands of tons of bombs were dropped on that country (equivalent to five times the power of the atomic bomb that destroyed Hiroshima), and its prolonged aftermath of severe sanctions gave rise to a humanitarian disaster that went virtually unreported. According to a 1999 UNICEF report, about half a million children under the age of five died in Iraq between 1991 and 1998 following the sanctions imposed on that country. The three United Nations Humanitarian Coordinators resigned, and one of them, Denis Halliday, described the sanctions as *genocide*.

Another dramatic example of insensitivity, among many, is the destruction in August 1998 of the largest pharmaceutical plant in Sudan, one of the poorest countries in the world. This resulted in a huge increase in mortality among the population, especially in children, whose diseases could not be treated because there were no medicines.

Fisk (2005, p. 505) reminds us that the worst act of terrorism in the Middle East occurred nineteen years before the attack on the Twin Towers: on 16 September 1982, Israel's ally the Lebanese Phalangist militia embarked on a three-day orgy of rape and killing in the Sabra and Chatila refugee camps. This episode took place after the Israeli invasion that was intended to expel the PLO from Lebanon—an operation endorsed by the US Administration—which cost the lives of 17,000 Lebanese and Palestinians, almost all of them civilians. This is five times the number of victims of 9/11. Fisk wonders why there should be such a difference in emotional reactions and psychological involvement between the attack on the World Trade Center in New York and the vast number of humanitarian tragedies that are passed over in silence, such as those of

Iraq, Sudan, or Palestine. There is no doubt that the Western media as a whole are fundamentally instrumental in facilitating such denial. While the pictures of the planes smashing into the Twin Towers have been shown on our television screens time and time again, we have seen nothing of the deaths of children or the wailing of mothers in the humanitarian catastrophes unleashed by senseless political responses. We need only imagine the reaction of Muslim terrorist sympathizers living in the West when they witness on television the anonymity of the portrayal of Palestinian fatalities compared with the highly dramatized depiction of Western deaths or victims of attacks in Israel. The conformism of the Western media, often attributable to ignorance of the specificity of peoples seemingly remote from us, also contributes to the radicalization of small groups of Muslims resident in the West, inducing them to embrace the terrorist option (Khosrokhavar, 2003).

When we distinguish between "them" (in this case, peoples outside the common ground of Western society) and "us", the former come to seem so alien that they disappear from our consciousness as human beings. A destructive act that would arouse horror if we were its victims moves us much less if inflicted on the enemy.

The opposing side's media of course influence public opinion in the relevant countries in like manner when they bombard viewers with harrowing images unseen on Western screens. This leaves no possibility of empathy with the suffering of peoples belonging to cultures different from one's own, so that anger is not aroused by criminal acts committed against the other side. The paranoid–schizoid manifestations occurring in this context result in the dehumanization of entire communities, so that wicked crimes are no longer seen as such and the destructive nature of the events concerned goes unremarked.

In writing this book, I myself progressed from an initial position of bewilderment and alarm at the phenomenon of suicide terrorism to a recognition that this form of present-day barbarism is merely one of the symptoms of the insanity that pervades the daily lives of millions of human beings.

In describing the processes of dehumanization that transform the enemy into an utterly diabolical and bad entity, the British psychoanalyst Hanna Segal (1997) stresses that the inability to take responsibility and experience guilt for destructive acts is a central factor in keeping mechanisms of triumph alive. In this author's view, super-identification with, and idealization of, the prevailing culture of the political elite may be important factors in the disavowal of violence committed by our own side and our indifference to it. If by definition we regard "civilized society" as engaged in a relentless struggle against evil and we have a cast-iron sense of right and wrong, then it is impossible for us even to ask ourselves whether we are capable of committing crimes against humanity. Such acts are deemed the prerogative of the enemy. (More than two centuries ago, Hume (1739–1940) observed that, when "our own nation is at war with any other, we detest them under the character of cruel, perfidious, unjust, and violent: but always esteem ourselves and our allies equitable, moderate, and merciful".)

Lussana (2002) points out that the fundamentalist position is based on the claim to be always in the right, and wonders whether the military and economic domination of the USA over poor and backward countries might perhaps make the attacks on the World Trade Center and the Pentagon more understandable (albeit not justifiable). Was it not the logic of retaliation that drove many American citizens to justify President Bush's decision to invade Iraq—an attack that gave rise to an exponential increase in acts of terrorism, especially by suicide bombers?

Conclusions

Acording to the evidence presented in this book, the majority of those who volunteer for suicide missions do so spontaneously: it is the individual who asks to sacrifice himself. Even the allegations about Chechen women being blackmailed into choosing martyrdom mostly prove to be unfounded: only one such case appears to have been confirmed, and was inflated by the Russian press. Another established finding is that the wish to die does not suffice in order for a terrorist act to be performed. Whenever someone who has decided to take his own life for personal reasons is deployed for a suicide mission, the attack fails: a melancholic who wants to end his life cannot bring himself to kill other people, for taking them with him to the grave would only increase his sense of guilt.[15]

If suicide bombers cannot be accommodated in any psychopathological category and if, as it appears, they are "normal" individuals, it must be concluded that their act is triggered by the extreme, desperate conditions in which they feel they are living. The diagnostic categories useful for the classification of certain psychopathological conditions cannot be applied to persons living in humiliation, who have been expelled from their homeland, or for whom the violent deaths of family members and friends are a matter of daily experience. This situation constitutes a specific traumatic state in which the wish to die in the name of the suffering and tragedy of the community as a whole assumes the concrete form of vengeful martyrdom. It is not easy for us in the West, with our cushioned existence, to understand this dramatic background.

The irreparable harm suffered by the suicide terrorist-to-be lies in the utter destruction of his affective world and of the objects that confer meaning on his existence. In extreme traumatic situations, where devastation is a daily fact of life, splitting and oblivion are not effective instruments for detachment from pain. The suffering is so intense that, for some, death is felt to be a liberation. Taking the enemy to the grave with them becomes a way of exacting vengeance and of making the other side experience what the victims have felt. As we have seen, a plight that fails to meet with a human response finds an omnipotent container in religious ideology.

With the spread of terrorism throughout the world, destructiveness has taken on an unprecedented aspect that we ourselves are ill-prepared to confront. What happened in the past at the hands of the Nazis, overwhelming an unprepared Europe, is now the chosen approach of international terrorism. Contemporary terrorism manifestly represents a step change in the quality of aggressive relations between peoples; it is an entirely new phenomenon on which it is not easy to reflect.

In this book, I have sought to emphasize that the specific factor in the phenomenon of suicide terrorism is the pathological union of individual suffering with the omnipotent, destructive mentality of the political or religious organization. The individual suffering that results in suicide martyrdom belongs to the *traumas of war*, and might go no further if the traumatized subjects did not succumb to the allure of the terrorist organization and were not attracted by fundamentalist propaganda or their community's culture of death. It is precisely the political organization that constitutes the *destructive network*, a structure that is not only well organized and whose tentacles extend throughout society, but which is also capable of constantly devising tactical actions, of which the martyrs are one resource, for a strategic end.

If we as psychoanalysts are to concern ourselves with terrorism, we must first of all eschew the facile solution of classifying the phenomenon in conventional paradigms. The risk that confronts us is that, given the *unthinkability of the events concerned*, no one will be able to suggest explanations whereby they might be contained and transformed. Split off and dissociated from consciousness, such a threat will inevitably constitute an ongoing source of anxiety and hate. By attempting to see the phenomenon of suicide terrorism in this way, we shall only be able to repress the event, while remaining unable to formulate questions to facilitate its understanding; the only response will then be that of an indiscriminate military counter-offensive.

An aggressive response such as that unleashed on Iraq after 9/11 elevated the conflict to a new level and ultimately played into the hands of the terrorists, whose policy was to create a state of emergency and widespread instability. The failure of the so-called *war on terror* has been borne out by the daily slaughter in Iraq, the country which was supposed to be pacified and democratized by the military intervention, but which has instead witnessed a huge increase in suicide attacks and violence on all sides.

It should not be forgotten that the failure to resolve the Israel–Palestine conflict has constituted another wound whereby the seeds of terrorism have been sown throughout the world. An equally worrying situation is that of Afghanistan, where, in the absence of a genuine political response to the country's problems, guerrilla warfare has gone from strength to strength and suicide martyrs have begun to appear.

It is difficult to predict at this juncture whether and when the spiral of destructiveness, which constantly fans the flames of hate, will come to an end and leave scope for the possibility of acknowledging the need for different identities to coexist. Given the spread of blind destruction, we are all called upon to champion the cause of constructiveness and life against the forces of cynicism and disintegration. The danger can only increase if we yield to the enticements of terrorism or respond simply by demonizing it and attempting to repress it by military means (thereby ultimately strengthening it). When faced with terrorism and counter-terrorist violence, we risk becoming passive spectators of the onslaught on the structures of human society. We may then even come to accept

the idea of being engaged in an irreversible clash of civilizations—
a conviction perhaps even more dangerous than that which
prevailed at the time of the nuclear threat, against which, however,
thousands mobilized.

While terrorism is one of the evils of our time, a pathological
response to the power relationships and imbalances of the contemporary world, it must be acknowledged that the phenomenon has
extremely remote origins. We must not only consider its cruelty and
devastating effects, but also be aware of the means at our disposal
for reducing and containing it in the future. In freeing ourselves
from the distortions that seek to persuade us that our customs,
democracy, and technology are the mark of a superior civilization,
we should once again embrace our traditional values of the fellow-
ship of all mankind.

This state of affairs is unlikely to be remedied in the short term
and its resolution will surely be left to future generations. However,
until the problems that underlie terrorism are solved, there will
always be candidates for martyrdom. If and when we witness the
establishment of less troubled societies, which are not racked by
suffering and trauma, and if and when a more equitable military
and economic balance is achieved between nations, it may be hoped
that this phenomenon can be consigned to history.

That will put an end to an appalling episode in which sacrificial
death was a stage in the process of mutual recognition between
peoples.

NOTES

1. Definitions of the phenomenon vary even between relatively homogeneous institutions. The United States Department of State defines terrorism as "premeditated, politically motivated violence perpetrated against noncombatant targets by subnational groups or clandestine agents" (Title 2 of the US Code, Chapter 38, Section 2656f(d)). The FBI's definition, however, is "the unlawful use of force and violence against persons or property to intimidate or coerce a government, the civilian population, or any segment thereof, in furtherance of political or social objectives".

2. Arousing indiscriminate anxiety is also the aim of terrorist attacks perpetrated by mad organizations, such as the 1995 incident on the Tokyo underground railway, when members of the Aum religious cult released a powerful nerve gas, sarin, in trains, causing twelve deaths and serious after-effects in thousands of other victims. This sect too, which had a hierarchical, pyramidal structure, had the ultimate objective of seizing power in Japan and the world. An interesting book by Haruki Murakami (2000) presents accounts of the attack by victims and by members of the terrorist organization itself.

3. The Japanese suicide pilots (and also naval personnel) were called "kamikaze", which means *divine wind*, after the typhoon that destroyed the Mongol fleet that was about to invade Japan in 1281.

4. Such was the dramatic background to the early years of the poet John Donne in England: born into a Catholic family, he wrote that, for some of his co-religionists, true martyrdom lay in not being martyred.

5. Hirsch (1997) coined the term *postmemories* to describe the emotional experiences of the children of Holocaust survivors. It refers to the posthumous effects on an individual or an entire community of a trauma that occurred at least a generation earlier. Salberg (2005) considers that this happens when the trauma was unthinkable to the first generation.

6. A skilful fictional description of how such a process might unfold is given in John Updike's novel *Terrorist*.

7. An extreme example of the older generation sending young people to their deaths is contained in the "Spiritual Manual" found in Mohammed Atta's luggage after 9/11. Notwithstanding some residual doubts about the authenticity of this document, the Manual, anticipating all possible uncertainties in the mind of the suicide-to-be, supports him in his determination and tells him which prayers to recite to overcome any doubt. For an interesting commentary on the "Spiritual Manual", see Kippenberg and Seidensticker (2006).

8. The concept of emotional trauma, defined in this way, is in some respects analogous to Khan's notion of *cumulative trauma* (Khan, 1963); for this author, constant, repeated microtraumas are held to be just as pathogenic as large-scale traumas. My own aim here is to draw attention, in particular, to the existence of early distortions of *emotional communication* between parent and child, with adverse consequences for the child's development.

9. According to Klein, some individuals never attain the depressive position, but remain in the paranoid-schizoid position throughout their lives. They consequently fail to show any consideration for the persons to whom they relate, whom they tend to use only as objects of pleasure. Conversely, an individual who attains the depressive position can put himself into the other's shoes, understand what fellow human beings are feeling, and avoid causing them pain and suffering.

10. To explain the death of living cells, biology today invokes the concept of *cell suicide* (Ameisen, 1999). Death is seen as an active process triggered when the environment becomes unfavourable and the conditions for survival are no longer satisfied. This process may be likened to the psychological situation: mental life may also include a predisposition to seek death actively when living becomes unbearable, by means of self-destructive mechanisms potentially present in all of us.

The earlier the trauma and the more it affects vital elements, the more readily self-destructive mechanisms capable of being unleashed will develop.

11. Perversion coincides neither with aggression nor with hate, but is the absence of love, or indifference. Gratified destructiveness, which thrives in indifference and the absence of passion, is the nucleus of perversion. "Rape has nothing to do with impotence. Absolute domination of another body becomes a drug. You rape, torture, and murder for the sense of being the master of other people's fate," declared Angelo Izzo, the "Circeo" murderer who killed three women in Italy in a notorious case dating from 1975.

12. Translator's note: This essay does not appear to have been published in English. The quotation is here translated from the Italian edition.

13. A recent example of lack of empathy and refusal of recognition with the aim of promoting aggressive opposition between two states is the insistence of President Ahmadinejad of Iran on denying the historical truth of the Holocaust. He even convened an international conference in Teheran in order to clothe this colossal operation of historical revisionism in scientific garb. In my view, he cannot really have believed that the greatest tragedy in the history of mankind never occurred, but instead wanted to apply, in the most extreme form possible, the hallowed technique of lack of empathy for the suffering and traumatic heritage of the Jewish people. Apart from the immediate political purpose of repudiation of the Jewish State, this is an essential tactic for fuelling hatred and mutual refusal of recognition.

14. In his analysis of the destructive behaviour of the *radical loser*, Enzensberger (2005) mentions an amalgam of a death wish and a catastrophic sense of omnipotence. The greater the absurdity of the project, the more fanatically it is pursued. The real objective is not victory, but extermination, dissolution, collective suicide, and a horrific end.

15. This is another reason why suicide bombers cannot be regarded as sufferers from a mental disorder such as, for instance, depression, which has been extensively studied by both psychiatry and psychoanalysis. On the other hand, a person may commit suicide as a protest against war and political violence. This was done in the past by Buddhist priests over the Vietnam war and by Jan Palach in Prague in response to the Soviet invasion. A recent example is that of Malachi Ritscher, aged fifty-two, who set himself on fire in Chicago on 3 November 2006 as a protest against the American policy of aggression against Iraq and for peace. A contributory factor in his sacrifice was a

psychological state that had nothing to do with the reasons for his protest, according to his son, who claimed that his father was extremely depressed and had decided in this way to impart a meaning to his suicide.

REFERENCES

Akhtar, S. (2003). Dehumanization: origins, manifestations, and reme-
dies. In: S. Varvin & V. D. Volkan (Eds.), *Violence or Dialogue?
Psychoanalytic Insights on Terror and Terrorism* (pp. 131–145). London:
Karnac.

Allam, K. F. (2006). *La solitudine dell'occidente*. Milan: Rizzoli.

Amati Sas, S. (2002). *La violenza sociale traumatica: una sfida alla nostra
adattabilità inconscia*. International Conference "Clinical Sándor
Ferenczi", Turin, 18–21 July.

Ameisen, J.-C. (1999). *La sculpture du vivant: Le suicide cellulaire ou la mort
créatrice*. Paris: Seuil.

Anders, G. (2006). *L'odio è antiquato*. Turin: Bollati Boringhieri. [Original
German publication: Anders, G. (1985). Die Antiquiertheit des
Hassens. In: R. Kahle, H. Menzner & G. Vinnai (Eds.), *Hass. Die
Macht eines unerwünschten Gefühls* (pp. 11–32). Reinbek bei
Hamburg: Rowohlt.]

Anderson, W. H. (2004). Terrorism underlying causes. *The Intelligencer,*
14: 53–58.

Argo, N. (2006). Human bombs: rethinking religion and terror. *MIT
Center for International Studies*, April.

Aulagnier, P. (1986). *Un interprète en quête de sens*. Paris: Ramsay.

Aust, S., & Schnibben, C. (Eds.) (2002). *11 September: Geschichte eines
Terrorangriffs*. Stuttgart: DVA.

Awad, G. (2003). The minds and perceptions of "the others". In: S. Varvin & V. Volkan (Eds.), *Violence or Dialogue: Psychoanalytic Insights on Terror and Terrorism* (pp. 153–176). London: International Psychoanalytical Association.

Awad, G. (2006). Contributi psicoanalitici per una teoria unificata del terrorismo. In: P. Capozzi (Ed.), *Atti del convegno, Milano 13 maggio 2006* (pp. 59–89). Milan: Quaderni del Centro milanese di psicoanalisi Cesare Musatti.

Awad, G., Berman, E., Grieco, A., Peregrini, C., Pirani, M., & Usuelli, A. (2006). *Alle radici dell'odio. Un'analisi del fenomeno terrorismo.* Quaderno n. 10 del Centro Milanese di Psicoanalisi.

Balint, M. (1979). *The Basic Fault: Therapeutic Aspects of Regression.* London: Tavistock.

Beaumont, P. (2003). The lost children of Rafah. *Observer,* London, 9 February 2003.

Bell, R. M. (1985). *Holy Anorexia.* Chicago, IL: University of Chicago Press.

Berman, E. (2006). Valori e transfert nella discussione psicoanalitica sul terrorismo e la politica In: P. Capozzi (Ed.), *Atti del convegno, Milano 13 maggio 2006* (pp. 13–27). Milan: Quaderni del Centro milanese di psicoanalisi Cesare Musatti.

Bettini, R. (2003). *Delenda America. Iperterrorismo islamista e anomia internazionale.* Milan: FrancoAngeli.

Bion, W. (1962). *Learning from Experience.* London: Tavistock.

Bion, W. (1970). *Attention and Interpretation: A Scientific Approach to Insight in Psycho-Analysis and Groups.* London: Tavistock.

Bohleber, W. (2003). Collective phantasms, destructiveness, and terrorism. In: S. Varvin & V. D. Volkan (Eds.), *Violence or Dialogue? Psychoanalytic Insights on Terror and Terrorism* (pp. 111–130). London: Karnac.

Carrère, E. (2000). *The Adversary: A True Story of Murder and Deception,* L. Coverdale (Trans.). London: Bloomsbury.

Chiesa, M. (2002). Terrorism: psycho-political observations on shock and indifference. In: Further contributions relating to terrorism. *Bulletin of the British Psycho-Analytical Society,* 37: 46–57.

Chodorow, N. (2003). Hate, humiliation, and masculinity. In: S. Varvin & V. D. Volkan (Eds.), *Violence or Dialogue? Psychoanalytic Insights on Terror and Terrorism.* (pp. 94–107). London: Karnac.

De Masi, F. (1999). *The Sadomasochistic Perversion: The Entity and the Theories,* P. Slotkin (Trans.). London: Karnac, 2003.

De Masi, F. (2002). *Making Death Thinkable: A Psychoanalytic Contribution to the Problem of the Transience of Life*, P. Antinucci (Trans.). London: Free Association Books, 2004.

De Masi, F. (2006). *Vulnerability to Psychosis: A Psychoanalytic Study of the Nature and Therapy of the Psychotic State*, P. Slotkin and others (Trans.). London: Karnac, 2009.

el-Sarraj (2004). E. Interview, 28 January (in Italian). http://it.peace reporter.net/articolo/1732/Intervista+a+Eyad+El-Sarraj (accessed 20 September 2010).

Enzensberger, H. M. (2005). The radical loser, N. Grindell (Trans.). www.signandsight.com/features/493.html (accessed May 2010). Originally published in *Der Spiegel*, 7 November 2005.

Euripides (2008). *Euripedes' Medea*, D. A. Svarlien (Trans.), Introduction and notes by R. Mitchell-Boyask. Indianapolis, IN: Hackett.

Ferenczi, S. (1929). The unwelcome child and his death-instinct. *International Journal of Psychoanalysis*, 10: 125–129.

Feuerbach, L. (1989), *The Essence of Christianity*, G. Eliot (Trans.). Amherst, NY: Prometheus.

Fisk, R. (2005). *The Great War for Civilisation: The Conquest of the Middle East*. London: Harper Perennial.

Freud, S. (1920g). *Beyond the Pleasure Principle. S.E.*, 18: 7–64: London: Hogarth.

Gambetta, D. (Ed.) (2005). *Making Sense of Suicide Missions*. Oxford: Oxford University Press.

Ghazali, S. (2003). The story of Hiba, 19, a suicide bomber. Can the road-map put an end to all this? *Independent*, London, 27 May.

Grieco, A. (2006). Per noi significava essere liberi. Appunti da Stammheim da testi di Gudrun Ensslin e Ulrike Meuinhof In: P. Capozzi (Ed.), *Atti del convegno, Milano 13 maggio 2006* (pp. 59–89). Milan: Quaderni del Centro milanese di psicoanalisi Cesare Musatti.

Haffey, N. (1998). *The United Nations and International Efforts to Deal With Terrorism*. Washington, DC: Pew Case Studies in International Affairs.

Hassan, N. (2001). An arsenal of believers. Talking to the human bombs. *New Yorker*, 19 November.

Hirsch, M. (1997). *Photography, Narrative, and Postmemory*. Cambridge, MA: Harvard University Press.

Hoffman, B.(1998). *Inside Terrorism*. New York: Columbia University Press.

Horgan, J. (2003). The search for the terrorist personality. In: A. Silke (Ed.), *Terrorists, Victims and Society: Psychological Perspectives on Terrorism and its Consequences* (pp. 3–27). Chichester: John Wiley.

Hough, G. (2004). Does psychoanalysis have anything to offer an understanding of terrorism? (Panel report). *Journal of the American Psychoanalytic Association, 52*: 813–828.

Hume, D. (1739–1740). *A Treatise of Human Nature.* Charleston, SC: BiblioBazaar, 2006.

Kaës, R. (2005). *Il disagio del mondo moderno e la sofferenza del nostro tempo.* SPI, Giornate Italiane su "I disagi delle civiltà". Milan: Il Saggiatore.

Kernberg, O. (2003). Sanctioned social violence: a psychoanalytic view, Parts I and II. *International Journal of Psychoanalysis, 84*: 683–698, 953–968.

Kernberg, O. (2006). The pressing need to increase research in and on psychoanalysis. *International Journal of Psychoanalysis, 87*: 919–926.

Khadra, Y. (2006). *The Attack,* J. Cullen (Trans.) New York: Talese/Doubleday.

Khan, M. R. (1963). The concept of cumulative trauma. *Psychoanalytic Study of the Child, 18*: 286–306.

Khosrokhavar, F. (2003). *Suicide Bombers: Allah's New Martyrs,* D. Macey (Trans.). London: Pluto Press, 2005.

Kippenberg, H. G., & Seidensticker, T. (Eds.) (2006). *The 9/11 Handbook: Annotated Translation and Interpretation of the Attackers' Spiritual Manual.* London: Equinox.

Klein, M. (1946). Notes on some schizoid mechanisms. In: M. Khan (Ed.), *Envy and Gratitude and Other Works 1946-1963.* London: Hogarth, 1975.

Koran, the (n.d.). J. M. Rodwell (Trans.). London: Dent.

Kramer, M. (1990). The moral logic of Hizballah. In: W. Reich (Ed.), *Origins of Terrorism, Psychologies, Ideologies, Theologies, States Of Mind* (pp. 131–157). Washington, DC: Woodrow Wilson Center Press.

London, J. (1915). *The Star Rover.* New York: Prometheus.

Lussana, P. (2002). Appunti sul terrorismo: se è concepibile l'idea di curarlo, piuttosto che solo combatterlo per distruggerlo. *Rivista di Psicoanalisi, 48*: 183–192.

Margalit, A., & Buruma, I. (2002). Occidentalism: the west in the eyes of its enemies. *New York Review of Books,* 17 January.

Meltzer, D. (1973). *Sexual States of Mind.* Strathtay, Perthshire: Clunie Press.

Meneguz, G. (2005). Note sull'interpretazione psicoanalitica del terrorismo e del fenomeno dei *suicidi-bombers*. *Psicoterapia e Scienze Umane*, 39: 165–192.

Merari, A. (1990). The readiness to kill and die: suicidal terrorism in the Middle East. In: W. Reich (Ed.), *Origins of Terrorism, Psychologies, Ideologies, Theologies, States of Mind* (pp. 192–209). Washington, DC: Woodrow Wilson Center Press.

Merari, A. (2002). Deterring fear: Government responses to terrorist attacks. *Harvard International Review*, 23: 26–31.

Miller, A. (1980). *For Your Own Good: Hidden Cruelty in Child-Rearing and the Roots of Violence*, H. & H. Hannum (Trans.). London: Faber, 1983.

Morris, I. (1975). *The Nobility of Failure: Tragic Heroes in the History of Japan*. London: Secker & Warburg.

Moussaoui, A. S., & Bouquillat, F. (2002). *Zacarias Moussaoui: The Making of a Terrorist*, S. Pleasance & F. Woods (Trans.). London: Serpent's Tail, 2003.

Murakami, H. (2000). *Underground*, A. Birnbaum & P. Gabriel (Trans.). New York: Vintage Books.

National Research Council (2002). *Discouraging Terrorism: Some Implications of 9/11*. Washington, DC: National Research Council.

Oliver, A. M., & Steinberg, P. F. (2005). *The Road to Martyrs' Square: A Journey into the World of the Suicide Bomber*. New York: Oxford University Press.

Pape, R. (2003). The strategic logic of suicide terrorism. *American Political Science Review*, 97: 21–42.

Peregrini, C. (2006). Terrorismo: considerazioni psicoanalitiche. In: P. Capozzi (Ed.), *Atti del convegno, Milano 13 maggio 2006* (pp. 27–43). Milan: Quaderni del Centro milanese di psicoanalisi Cesare Musatti.

Pirani, M. (2006). Gli occhiali biblici. In P. Capozzi (Ed.), *Atti del convegno, Milano 13 maggio 2006* (pp. 111–121). Milan: Quaderni del Centro milanese di psicoanalisi Cesare Musatti.

Post, J. (1984). Notes on a psychodynamic theory of terrorist behavior. *Terrorism: An International Journal*, 7: 241–256.

Post, J. (1990). Terrorist psycho-logic: terrorist behavior as a product of psychological forces. In: W. Reich (Ed.), *Origins of Terrorism, Psychologies, Ideologies, Theologies, States Of Mind* (pp. 25–40). Washington, DC: Woodrow Wilson Center Press.

Puget, J. (1995). Psychic reality or various realities. *International Journal of Psychoanalysis*, 76: 29–34.

Rascovsky, A. (1973). *Filicide: The Murder, Humiliation, Mutilation, Denigration, and Abandonment of Children by Parents*, S. Hale Rogers (Trans.). Northvale, NJ: Jason Aronson, 1995.

Reuter, C. (2002). *My Life is a Weapon: A Modern History of Suicide Bombing*, H. Ragg-Kirkby (Trans.). Princeton, NJ: Princeton University Press.

Rizzolatti, G., & Gallese, V. (1998). From action to meaning: a neurophysiological perspective. In: J. L. Petit (Ed.), *Les neurosciences et la philosophie de l'action*. Paris: Librairie Philosophique J. Vrin.

Robins, R., & Post, J. (1997). *Political Paranoia: The Psychopolitics of Hatred*. New Haven, CT: Yale University Press.

Rosenfeld, H. A. (1971). A clinical approach to the psychoanalytic theory of the life and death instinct: an investigation into the aggressive aspects of narcissism. *International Journal of Psychoanalysis, 52*: 169–178.

Rosenfeld, H. A. (1978). Notes on the psychopathology and psychoanalytic treatment of some borderline patients. *International Journal of Psychoanalysis, 59*: 215–221.

Sade, D.-A.-F. de (1784). The one hundred and twenty days of Sodom. In: *The One Hundred and Twenty Days of Sodom and Other Writings*, A. Wainhouse & R. Seaver (Comp. & Trans.). London: Arrow, 1991.

Sageman, M. (2004). *Understanding Terror Networks*. Philadelphia, PA: University of Pennsylvania Press.

Salberg, J. (2005). Études on loss. *American Imago, 6*: 435–452.

Schelling, T. (1966). *Arms and Influence*. New Haven, CT: Yale University Press.

Schmitt, C. (2007). *Theory of the Partisan*, G. L. Ulmen (Trans.). New York: Telos Press.

Schweitzer, Y. (2001). Suicide bombings: the ultimate weapon? ICT: http://www.ict.org.il/Articles/tabid/66/Articlsid/68/currentpage/26/Default.aspx (accessed September 2010).

Schweitzer, Y. (2006). Palestinian female suicide bombers: reality vs. myth. In: Y. Schweitzer (Ed.), *Female Suicide Bombers: Dying for Equality?* (pp. 25–42). Memorandum No. 84, Jaffee Center for Strategic Studies (JCSS).

Segal, H. (1997). From Hiroshima to the Gulf and after: socio-political expressions of ambivalence. In: J. Steiner (Ed.), *Psychoanalysis, Literature and War: Papers 1972–1995* (pp. 129–138). London: Routledge.

Seidensticker, T. (2006). The religious and historical background of suicide attacks in the name of Islam. In: H. G. Kippenberg &

T. Seidensticker (Eds.). *The 9/11 Handbook: Annotated Translation and Interpretation of the Attackers' Spiritual Manual*. London: Equinox.

Sen, A. (2006). *Identity and Violence: The Illusion of Destiny*. London: Allen Lane.

Silke, A. (2003). Becoming a terrorist. In: A. Silke (Ed.), *Terrorists, Victims and Society: Psychological Perspectives on Terrorism and its Consequences* (pp. 29–54). Chichester: John Wiley.

Speckhard, A. (2005). Understanding suicide terrorism: countering human bombs and their senders. In: J. S. Purcell & J. D. Weintraub (Eds.), *Topics in Terrorism: Toward a Transatlantic Consensus on the Nature of the Threat* (Vol. 1). Washington, DC: Atlantic Council Publication.

Speckhard, A. (2006). Suicide terrorism, genesis of. In: G. Fink (Ed.), *Encyclopedia of Stress*. Oxford: Elsevier.

Speckhard, A., & Akhmedova, K. (2004). Mechanisms of generating suicide terrorism: trauma and bereavement as psychological vulnerabilities in human security—the Chechen case. www.anne speckhard.com/publications/Suicide_Terrorism_Chechen_Case. pdf (accessed 3 May 2011).

Speckhard, A., & Akhmedova, K. (2006a). The making of a martyr: Chechen suicide terrorism. *Journal of Studies in Conflict and Terrorism, 29*(5): 1–65.

Speckhard, A., & Akhmedova, K. (2006b). Black widows: the Chechen female suicide terrorists. In: Y. Schweitzer (Ed.), *Female Suicide Bombers: Dying for Equality?* (pp. 63–80). Memorandum No. 84, Jaffee Center for Strategic Studies (JCSS).

Sophocles (1893). *Antigone*, R. C. Jebb (Trans.).

Stapley, L. F. (2006). *Globalization and Terrorism: Death of a Way of Life*. London: Karnac.

Stein, R. (2002). Evil as love and as liberation. *Psychoanalytic Dialogues, 12*: 393–420.

Touraine, A. (1997). *Pourrons-nous vivre ensemble? Egaux et différents*. Paris: Fayard.

Twemlow, S. W., & Sacco, F. C. (2002). Reflections on the making of a terrorist. In: C. Covington, P. Williams, J. Arundale,k & J. Knox (Eds.), *Terrorism and War: Unconscious Dynamics of Political Violence* (pp. 97–123). London: Karnac.

Updike, J. (2006). *Terrorist*. New York: Alfred Knopf.

Usuelli, A. (2006). Riflessioni sul terrorismo. In: P. Capozzi (Ed.), *Atti del convegno, Milano 13 maggio 2006* (pp. 89–111). Milan: Quaderni del Centro milanese di psicoanalisi Cesare Musatti.

Varvin, S. (2003). Terrorism and victimization: individual and large-group dynamics. In: S. Varvin & V. D. Volkan (Eds.), *Violence or Dialogue? Psychoanalytic Insights on Terror and Terrorism* (pp. 53–72). London: Karnac.

Varvin, S., & Volkan, V. (Eds.) (2003). *Violence or Dialogue? Psychoanalytic Insights on Terror and Terrorism.* London: Karnac.

Vedantam, S. (2003). When violence masquerades as virtue. In: S. Varvin & V. D. Volkan (Eds.), *Violence or Dialogue? Psychoanalytic Insights on Terror and Terrorism* (pp. 7–30). London: Karnac.

Volkan, S. (2003). Traumatized societies. In: S. Varvin & V. D. Volkan (Eds.), *Violence or Dialogue? Psychoanalytic Insights on Terror and Terrorism* (pp. 217–236). London: Karnac.

Winnicott, D. (1965). *The Family and Individual Development.* London: Tavistock.

Winnicott, D. (1971). *Playing and Reality.* London: Tavistock.

Wright, J. (2004). *The Jesuits: Missions, Myths and Histories.* London: HarperCollins.

INDEX